ONE MORE SLICE

LEILA LINDHOLM

Published in 2011 by New Holland Publishers (UK) Ltd
London Cape Town Sydney Auckland
www.newhollandpublishers.com
Garfield House, 86–88 Edgware Road, London W2 2EA, United Kingdom

80 McKenzie Street, Cape Town 8001, South Africa
Unit 1, 66 Gibbes Street, Shatswood, NSW 2067, Australia
218 Lake Road, Northcote, Auckland, New Zealand

First published by Walter and Books, Sweden,
in 2010 as *One More Slice*
© 2010 Leila Lindholm
© 2011 English translation, New Holland Publishers

A catalogue record for this book is available from the British Library

ISBN 978-1-78009-000-9

Publisher: Clare Sayer
Recipes, texts and food styling: Leila Lindholm
Production: Laurence Poos
Graphic design: Mikael Engblom
Photography: Wolfgang Kleinschmidt
Translator: B.J. Epstein
Reproduction by Pica Digital PTE Ltd (Singapore)
Printed and bound in Singapore by Tien Wah Press PTE Ltd

LEILA LINDHOLM

one more slice

Sourdough bread, pizza, pasta and sweet pastries

NEW HOLLAND

viva la famiglia!

I have always been close to my family and we spent a lot of time together when I was a child. Gathering around the dinner table was an unbeatable way of spending time together and these days I think it is more important than ever now that I have my own little family. My son has turned out to be a bon vivant and gourmand, just like his parents. He likes to eat a lot. It's so much fun cooking for him and it's getting more pleasurable now that he's learning to eat on his own. He happily tries new dishes and tests new flavours.

When I was little, I loved food and being in the kitchen. I especially remember how much fun it was to bake. It was like magic in the kitchen, seeing how a little flour, yeast, eggs and sugar could be transformed into fantastic pastries. It wasn't just sweet things that we baked, but also pizza and bread. Today I'm convinced that it is more important than ever for young people to discover the art of baking, and it can also be a fun experience to share with one's grandma or parents. In Italy, recipes are inherited and you guard and protect your family's recipes like the treasures they are. I think that baking can be a way of building bridges between generations and cultures. Try to pass on knowledge and delicious recipes from generation to generation but above all, get your apron on and have fun in the kitchen, and then enjoy the fruits of your labours.

My first cookbook, *A Piece of Cake*, was all about baking. My plan was always to write two books – the first focusing on sweet baked goods, such as cupcakes, cookies and cakes. This second book looks in detail at sourdough bread, pancakes and waffles, and even more 'hearty baking' such as pasta and pizza from scratch. I also wanted to cover sweets such as ice cream cakes, cheesecakes, brownies and blondies.

This book is the perfect basic guide for the home cook and will provide you with plenty of good recipes from which to choose. Is there anything better than making and having dinner together with family and friends?

Good luck in the kitchen!

Hugs
Leila

pizza amore

A really good pizza requires a good base, homemade tomato sauce and, of course, good cheese. I think that buffalo mozzarella is a must on an Italian pizza. Here are my best recipes for simple and yummy pizzas. Once they are baked, I usually drizzle a little olive oil over top and season with freshly ground black pepper and fresh herbs. Be careful with the salt, though, since some ingredients such as salami, ham or anchovies are salty themselves. To get a crispy, golden pizza, the oven must be really, really hot, around 250°C (500°F/gas 10). Use a pizza stone if possible (look in good kitchen equipment shops). The flat pizza stone goes into the oven to preheat, then the pizza is laid directly on top of the hot stone.

basic pizza dough

This pizza dough works well when there isn't much time for baking. While the dough is rising, you have time to prepare the filling. The base turns wonderfully crispy and the edges become beautifully bubbly. You can cold-rise the dough overnight.

BASIC RECIPE
MAKES 4 LARGE PIZZAS
15 g (½ oz) fresh yeast
300 ml (10 fl oz) lukewarm water
2 tsp sugar
1 tsp sea salt
2 tbsp olive oil
75 g (3 oz) durum wheat flour
350–400 g (12–14 oz) strong bread
    flour

1. Crumble the yeast in a bowl and dissolve in the water. Add the sugar, salt and olive oil.
2. Add the two flours a little at a time and knead the dough in a mixer for around 10 minutes, until it is elastic. (You can also knead the dough by hand.)
3. Sprinkle a little flour over the dough, cover with a cloth and leave to rise in the bowl for about 45 minutes, until it is double in size. While the dough is rising, preheat the oven to 250°C (500°F/gas 10).
4. Divide the dough into 4 and roll each one out thinly on a floured surface.
5. Add the filling of your choice (see the variations).
6. Bake in the middle of the oven for around 5 minutes.

pizza dough with sourdough starter

This makes a soft, elastic dough that is easy to work with. After it has risen, don't knead it again if you want air bubbles in the edges. This base has a strong taste, a good level of saltiness and it is wonderfully chewy and crisp at the edges.

BASIC RECIPE
MAKES 5 LARGE PIZZAS
12 g (⅓ oz) fresh yeast
300 ml (10 fl oz) cold water
3 tbsp olive oil
50 ml (2 fl oz) wheat sourdough starter
    (see recipe page 148)
1 tbsp salt
1 tsp sugar
200 g (7 oz) durum wheat flour
200 g (7 oz) strong bread flour

1. Crumble the yeast in a bowl and dissolve in the water. Add the olive oil, sourdough starter, salt and sugar.
2. Add the two flours a little at a time, then knead the dough in a mixer (or by hand) for about 10 minutes, until it is elastic.
3. Sprinkle a little flour over it and let the dough rise in the bowl under a cloth for about 2 hours, until it doubles in size.
4. Preheat the oven to 250°C (500°F/gas 10).
5. Divide the dough into 5 balls, place on a floured tray and cover with clingfilm. Either rest in the refrigerator overnight or roll out until paper-thin on a floured surface
6. Add the filling of your choice (see the variations).
7. Bake the pizzas in the middle of the oven for around 5 minutes or until done.

tomato sauce for pizza

It is always tastiest when you make your own tomato sauce. Try to use really sweet, sun-ripened tomatoes; alternatively use cherry tomatoes on the vine.

BASIC RECIPE
MAKES SAUCE FOR 4 LARGE PIZZAS
2 garlic cloves, finely chopped
5 ripe tomatoes, finely diced
1 tbsp butter
1 tbsp honey, clear
1 tsp white wine vinegar
sea salt
freshly ground black pepper

1. Melt the butter in a pan and lightly fry the peeled and finely chopped garlic.
2. Add the honey and diced tomato. Cook the sauce until the tomatoes are completely soft and the sauce has thickened, about 20 minutes.
3. Season with vinegar, salt and black pepper. Let cool.

pizza bread with garlic butter

MAKES 4 BREADS
1 portion pizza dough of your choice (see basic recipe, page 10)
2 garlic cloves, peeled and crushed
1 large bunch of parsley, finely chopped
100 g (4 oz) softened butter
flour, for sprinkling

1. Preheat the oven to 220°C (425°F/gas 7). Divide the dough into 4 pieces and roll each one out into a rectangle.
2. Mix the garlic and chopped parsley with the softened butter, and divide into 4 pats. Place a garlic butter pat in the centre of the rectangle
3. Fold the upper longer side into the middle and the lower one over it to make a parcel. Fold one of the shorter sides over to the other and pinch the ends together.
4. Cover and let it rise until double in size, then bake in the oven for 15–20 minutes.

pane musica

If you have leftover pizza dough or if the dough is about to over-ferment, you can make it into a very tasty bread. It is very quick to prepare and makes a good snack.

MAKES 6 BREADS
1 portion pizza dough of your choice (see basic recipe, page 10)
olive oil
sea salt
fresh rosemary, finely chopped

1. Preheat the oven to 220°C (425°F/gas 7). Divide the dough into 6 pieces and roll each one out really thinly.
2. Place them on a baking tray lined with baking parchment.
3. Drizzle well with olive oil, sprinkle with sea salt and the finely chopped rosemary.
4. Bake in the middle of the oven for about 5 minutes, until golden bubbles appear on the surface.

a dozen savoury pizzas

When making pizzas it is important to use really good ingredients. Don't forget to add seasoning to your pizza, but take it easy with the salt if you are using salty cheeses or prosciutto that is naturally salty. It is important to only spread a thin layer of sauce on the pizza, otherwise the base will get soggy and it will be hard to lift your uncooked pizza over to the oven.

pizza with asparagus and goats' cheese

MAKES 4 LARGE PIZZAS

1 portion pizza dough of your choice
    (see page 10)
1 portion tomato sauce (see page 13)
1 bunch green asparagus spears
250 g (9 oz) goats' cheese (chèvre)
250 g (9 oz) buffalo mozzarella cheese
100 g (4 oz) black olives, stoned
5 sprigs of fresh rosemary, finely
    chopped
freshly ground black pepper
olive oil

1. Preheat the oven to 250°C (500°F/gas 10).
2. Make the pizza dough and tomato sauce according to the basic recipes. Divide dough into 4 pieces.
3. Remove the lower woody stalks of the asparagus, then boil the spears for about 2 minutes. Cool in ice water and then cut into bite-sized pieces.
4. Roll out the dough thinly and spread with a scant layer of tomato sauce.
5. Crumble the goats' cheese, tear up the mozzarella and scatter both over the pizzas. Sprinkle with olives, asparagus pieces and rosemary then season with black pepper.
6. Bake in the middle of the oven for 5–10 minutes.
7. Drizzle with olive oil before serving.

calzone

MAKES 2 LARGE CALZONES

1 portion pizza dough of your choice
    (see page 10)
200 g (7 oz) smoked ham
250 g (9 oz) buffalo mozzarella cheese
1 bunch of fresh oregano, leaves
    removed from stalks and chopped
150 g (5 oz) Parmesan cheese, grated
2 handfuls black olives, stoned and
    chopped

1. Preheat the oven to 250°C (500°F/gas 10).
2. Make the pizza dough according to the basic recipe.
3. Cube the ham and slice the mozzarella.
4. Divide the dough into two pieces. Roll each piece out thinly and sprinkle half the ham, cheese, oregano and olives onto half of each rolled-out piece. Brush a little water around the edges and fold the circles in half. Pinch the edges together.
5. Bake the calzones in the middle of the oven for 5–10 minutes.

pizza bianca

This pizza is white because the tomato sauce is replaced with spreadable ricotta cheese. It is really delicious and you can make it in record time!

MAKES 4 LARGE PIZZAS

1 portion pizza dough of your choice
   (see page 10)
250 g (9 oz) ricotta cheese
50 g (2 oz) Parmesan cheese, grated
250 g (9 oz) buffalo mozzarella cheese
50 g (2 oz) pine nuts
4 garlic cloves, thinly sliced
4 sprigs of rosemary, finely chopped
olive oil for drizzling

1. Preheat the oven to 250°C (500°F/gas 10).
2. Make the pizza dough according to the basic recipe and divide into 4 pieces.
3. Roll the dough out thinly and spread with a layer of ricotta cheese. Grate Parmesan over it and place slices of mozzarella and pine nuts on top.
4. Sprinkle chopped garlic and rosemary over the pizzas, drizzle with a little olive oil and season with salt and pepper.
5. Bake the pizzas in the middle of the oven for 5–10 minutes.

pizza ai funghi

MAKES 4 LARGE PIZZAS

1 portion pizza dough of your choice
   (see page 10)
1 portion tomato sauce (see page 13)
3 large porcini mushrooms, thinly
   sliced
2 tbsp butter
375 g (13 oz) buffalo mozzarella cheese
4 garlic cloves, thinly sliced
1 bunch of fresh parsley, finely
   chopped
4 sprigs fresh rosemary, finely
   chopped
olive oil for drizzling

1. Preheat the oven to 250°C (500°F/gas 10).
2. Make the pizza dough and tomato sauce according to the basic recipes, and divide into 4 pieces.
3. Fry the mushrooms in the butter until golden brown and season. Slice the mozzarella.
4. Roll the dough out thinly and spread with a scant layer of tomato sauce. Distribute the fried mushrooms, garlic and mozzarella over the pizzas. Top with parsley and rosemary.
5. Bake in the middle of the oven for 5–10 minutes.
6. Once done, drizzle each pizza with a little olive oil and season with salt and pepper.

pizza ai quattro formaggi

MAKES 4 LARGE PIZZAS

1 portion pizza dough of your choice
   (see page 10)
1 portion tomato sauce (see page 13)
400 g (14 oz) mixed cheeses (Taleggio,
   Fontina, Parmesan, Gorgonzola)
150 g (5 oz) walnuts, chopped

1. Preheat the oven to 250°C (500°F/gas 10).
2. Make the pizza dough and tomato sauce according to the basic recipes and divide into 4 pieces.
3. Grate the hard cheeses and divide the Gorgonzola and Taleggio. Roll the dough out thinly, spread with a scant layer of tomato sauce on each pizza. Sprinkle with the cheeses and coarsely chopped walnuts.
4. Bake the pizzas in the middle of the oven for 5–10 minutes.

pizza al salame

MAKES 4 LARGE PIZZAS

1 portion pizza dough of your choice
(see page 10)
1 portion tomato sauce (see page 13)
1 aubergine, thinly sliced
4 garlic cloves, thinly sliced
1 mild red chilli, thinly sliced
375 g (13 oz) buffalo mozzarella
cheese, sliced
150 g (5 oz) salami
1 bunch of fresh oregano, leaves
stripped from branches
olive oil for drizzling

1. Preheat the oven to 250°C (500°F/gas 10).
2. Make the pizza dough and tomato sauce according to the basic recipes. Divide dough into 4 pieces.
3. Fry the sliced aubergine well in plenty of olive oil.
4. Roll the 4 pieces of dough out thinly and spread with a scant layer of tomato sauce.
5. Layer the salami, aubergine, chilli, mozzarella and oregano on each pizza.
6. Bake the pizzas in the middle of the oven for 5–10 minutes.
7. Once done, drizzle with a little olive oil and season with salt and pepper.

pizza alla capricciosa

MAKES 4 LARGE PIZZAS

1 portion pizza dough of your choice
(see page 10)
1 portion tomato sauce (see page 13)
150 g (5 oz) smoked ham,
1 ripe tomato, thinly sliced
250 g (9 oz) mushrooms, thinly sliced
4 garlic cloves, thinly sliced
375 g (13 oz) buffalo mozzarella cheese
1 bunch of fresh basil
olive oil for drizzling

1. Preheat the oven to 250°C (500°F/gas 10).
2. Make the pizza dough and tomato sauce according to the basic recipes. Divide dough into 4 pieces
3. Roll out each piece of dough thinly and spread with a scant layer of tomato sauce.
4. Slice the mozzarella. Distribute the ham, cheese, tomato and mushrooms over the pizzas along with some of the whole basil leaves.
5. Bake the pizzas in the middle of the oven for 5–10 minutes.
6. When done, drizzle over a little olive oil, some freshly ground black pepper and garnish with a few more basil leaves.

pizza ai carciofi

MAKES 4 LARGE PIZZAS

1 portion pizza dough of your choice
(see page 10)
1 portion tomato sauce (see page 13)
2 tins artichoke hearts
olive oil
250 g (9 oz) Pecorino cheese, grated
100 g (4 oz) walnuts, roughly chopped
1 bunch of fresh thyme, leaves stripped
from stalks

1. Preheat the oven to 250°C (500°F/gas 10).
2. Make the pizza dough and tomato sauce according to the basic recipes. Divide the dough into 4 pieces.
3. Drain the artichokes well and fry them in olive oil until nicely browned.
4. Roll out each piece of dough thinly and spread with a scant layer of tomato sauce.
5. Distribute the artichokes, Pecorino and walnuts over the bases. Season with salt and freshly ground black pepper.
6. Bake the pizzas in the middle of the oven for 5–10 minutes.
7. When done, drizzle with a little olive oil. Top with thyme.

pizza alla caprese

This wonderfully thin crusted pizza has a double dose of tomato in the list of ingredients – not only does the base have a thin coating of tomato sauce, I have also used as many varieties of tomato as I could get my hands on. Try it yourself during the summer months when the markets are full of interesting varieties of tomato.

MAKES 4 LARGE PIZZAS

1 portion pizza dough of your choice (see page 10)

1 portion tomato sauce (see page 13)

375 g (13 oz) buffalo mozzarella cheese, sliced

6 tomatoes (different colours), sliced

4 garlic cloves, thinly sliced

1 bunch of fresh basil

olive oil for drizzling

1. Preheat the oven to 250°C (500°F/gas 10).
2. Make the pizza dough and tomato sauce according to the basic recipes. Divide dough into 4 pieces.
3. Roll out the 4 peices of dough thinly and spread with a scant layer of tomato sauce.
4. Distribute the mozzarella, tomatoes and garlic over the pizzas. Scatter over some whole basil leaves.
5. Bake the pizzas in the middle of the oven for 5–10 minutes.
6. When done, drizzle over a little olive oil, black pepper and garnish with a few more basil leaves.

pizza al proschiutto e fiche

These mini pizzas are great for a party. I serve well-chilled beer, sparkling or red wine with these tasty fresh fig, prosciutto and chilli pizzas.

MAKES 16 MINI PIZZAS

1 portion pizza dough of your choice (see page 10)

1 portion tomato sauce (see page 13)

375 g (13 oz) buffalo mozzarella cheese, sliced

5 fresh figs, sliced

1 mild red chilli, thinly sliced

150 g (5 oz) prosciutto, thinly sliced

1 bunch of fresh thyme, leaved removed from stalks

olive oil for drizzling

1. Preheat the oven to 250°C (500°F/gas 10).
2. Make the pizza dough and tomato sauce according to the basic recipes. Divide dough into 16 pieces.
3. Roll out the 16 pieces of dough thinly and spread each with a scant layer of tomato sauce.
4. Layer the ingredients over the pizzas and season with thyme, sea salt and freshly ground pepper.
5. Bake the pizzas until golden in the middle of the oven for 5–10 minutes. Watch carefully so they don't overcook.
6. When done, drizzle a little olive oil over each mini pizza.

pizza sticks with feta

This tasty snack is super-easy to make and perfect for a cocktail party. Slice the pizza into slender canapé sizes and serve the sticks warm with drinks or a good wine.

MAKES ABOUT 20 STICKS

½ portion pizza dough of your choice
    (see page 10)
200 g (7 oz) feta cheese, crumbled
few sprigs of fresh rosemary, leaves
    removed and finely chopped
sea salt
2 tbsp honey, clear
olive oil for drizzling

1. Preheat the oven to 250°C (500°F/gas 10).
2. Make the pizza dough according to the basic recipe. Divide into 2 pieces.
3. Roll out the dough thinly into two oblong pizza bases.
4. Distribute the feta and rosemary over the pizzas. Sprinkle with sea salt and drizzle with honey and olive oil.
5. Bake the pizzas in the oven for around 5 or so minutes.
6. When done, slice the pizzas into sticks.

pizza pinwheels

Pizza pinwheels are the perfect accompaniment to drinks – small and tasty to nibble. Sardines and Parmesan offer saltiness, but aren't overly fishy tasting. When you slice the roll, the pinwheels press together and become oblong so ease the slices back into a round shape before placing them in the oven.

100 SMALL PINWHEELS

1 portion pizza dough of your choice
   (see page 10)

2 garlic cloves, crushed

1 bunch of fresh oregano, leaves
   removed and finely chopped

2 sardine fillets

200 g (7 oz) butter, softened

200 g (7 oz) Parmesan cheese, finely
   grated

water for brushing

sea salt

1. Preheat the oven to 250°C (500°F/gas 10).
2. Make the pizza dough according to the basic recipe and let it rise. Divide the dough into 2 pieces.
3. Mash the sardine fillets; mix these and the garlic, oregano and three-quarters of the Parmesan with the softened butter.
4. Roll the dough out into two thin rectangles. Spread the butter over the 2 rectangles and sprinkle over the rest of the cheese. Brush the edge of one of the long sides with a little water.
5. Roll the dough into a tight roll from the other long side.
6. Slice the dough into thin slices with a sharp knife and place the pinwheels on a tray lined with baking parchment. Sprinkle with a little sea salt.
7. Bake until golden in the middle of the oven for 10 minutes.

five sweet pizzas

I make my sweet pizzas with ricotta and mascarpone cheeses and top them with fresh berries, fruit, chocolate, almonds and other nuts. Just like other pizzas, they can be varied to suit your personal tastes.

mascarpone pizza with fresh peaches

Mascarpone cheese is a creamy cows' milk cheese and it is often used in Italian desserts – the most well known of which are tiramisu and mascarpone-filled cannoli.

MAKES 1 PIZZA
¼ portion pizza dough (see page 10)
125 g (4½ oz) ricotta cheese
125 g (4½ oz) mascarpone cheese
50 g (2 oz) almond paste, grated
finely grated zest of 1 lemon
75 g (3 oz) strawberries
75 g (3 oz) raspberries
2 peaches
25 g (1 oz) flaked almonds
50 g (2 oz) pistachios, coarsely
   chopped
1 tbsp demerara sugar
icing sugar, to decorate

1. Preheat the oven to 250°C (500°F/gas 10).
2. Make the pizza dough according to the basic recipe.
3. Roll the dough out thinly and spread with a layer of ricotta.
4. Top with mascarpone, then scatter the almond paste and lemon zest over it.
5. Slice the strawberries and peaches and distribute these and the raspberries over the pizza.
6. Sprinkle with almonds, pistachios and demerara sugar.
7. Bake in the middle of the oven for 5–10 minutes.
8. Dust with icing sugar before serving.

pear pizza with stilton

This awesomely good pizza can be served as a cheesy dessert or with the cheese tray. The sweet pears contrasted with the salty, creamy Stilton is delicious.

MAKES 8 SMALL PIZZAS
½ portion pizza dough of your choice
   (see page 10)
250 g (9 oz) ricotta cheese
4 large pears, thinly sliced
300 g (10 oz) Stilton cheese, crumbled
50 g (2 oz) walnuts, coarsely chopped

1. Preheat the oven to 250°C (500°F/gas 10).
2. Make the pizza dough according to the basic recipe and divide into 8 pieces.
3. Roll the dough out thinly and spread a layer of ricotta on every pizza. Distribute the pears over the pizzas.
4. Crumble the Stilton over the pears, then sprinkle over the chopped walnuts.
5. Bake in the middle of the oven for 5–10 minutes.

pizza gino

This sweet and wonderfully tasty pizza is a variant of the classic Italian dessert *gino*, although with tons of fresh berries. White chocolate becomes meltingly delicious in the oven and with its slightly crispy texture, it perfectly suits the fresh berries.

MAKES 1 LARGE PIZZA

¼ portion pizza dough of your choice (see page 10)
125 g (4½ oz) ricotta cheese
200 g (7 oz) mixed berries (strawberries, raspberries, blueberries, red currants)
50 g (2 oz) good quality white chocolate, coasely chopped
1 tbsp demerara sugar
icing sugar and fresh basil, to decorate

1. Preheat the oven to 250°C (500°F/gas 10).
2. Make the pizza dough according to the basic recipe.
3. Roll the dough out thinly and spread the base with a layer of ricotta cheese.
4. Slice the strawberries, then sprinkle them and the other berries over the pizza. Sprinkle the chopped white chocolate and demerara sugar over the berries.
5. Bake in the middle of the oven for 5–10 minutes.
6. Dust the pizza with icing sugar and garnish with fresh basil.

fig pizza with chocolate

These small pizzas are just right for a party. They are a perfect dessert, and are equally good with coffee or as an unusual brunch dish.

MAKES 24 MINI PIZZAS

1 portion pizza dough of your choice
   (see page 10)
500 g (¼ lb) ricotta cheese
finely grated zest of 2 oranges
150 g (5 oz) almond paste, grated
100 g (4 oz) good quality dark chocolate
   (70% cocoa solids), chopped
12 fresh figs, sliced
50 ml (2 fl oz) honey, clear

1. Preheat the oven to 250°C (500 °C/gas 10).
2. Make the pizza dough according to the basic recipe.
3. Divide the dough into 24 pieces and roll out into round mini pizzas. Place on trays lined with baking parchment.
4. Spread each with ricotta cheese and sprinkle with orange zest and almond paste over them.
5. Distribute the chocolate and figs over the pizzas, then drizzle a little clear honey over each.
6. Bake the pizzas in the middle of the oven for 8–10 minutes.

apple pizza with almonds

This pizza is reminiscent of the classic apple tarte tatin and is really good served with softened vanilla ice cream. I sometimes spice up this pizza with fresh chopped rosemary, which complements the apples and vanilla ice cream deliciously.

MAKES 8 SMALL PIZZAS

½ portion pizza dough of your choice
   (see page 10)
50 g (2 oz) butter for frying
8 small apples (or 4 large ones),
   peeled and cut into slices
3 tbsp sugar
1 tbsp cinnamon
250 g (9 oz) ricotta cheese
200 g (7 oz) almond paste, grated
50 g (2 oz) flaked almonds
icing sugar, to decorate

1. Preheat the oven to 250°C (500 °C/gas 10).
2. Make the pizza dough according to the basic recipe.
3. Fry the peeled and sliced apple segments until golden in the butter, sugar and cinnamon.
4. Roll the dough out thinly into 8 mini pizzas and spread with ricotta cheese. Sprinkle over the grated almond paste.
5. Distribute the fried apples over the pizzas and sprinkle with a few flaked almonds.
6. Bake in the middle of the oven for 5–10 minutes.
7. Dust with icing sugar before serving.

say cheesecake!

For me, cheesecake is the perfect cake – just the thought of this tasty pastry makes my mouth water. Cheesecake can be varied endlessly; it is perfect for dessert, with coffee and at a picnic in the summer. Here are my some of my favourites, which have become classics in my kitchen, both at home and in the country.

frozen cheesecake

Using a springform cake tin gives this dessert a slightly more finished look, but it will work just as well if made in a bowl or plastic container; in which case scoop the cheesecake into bowls to serve.

MAKES 1 CHEESECAKE/SERVES 8–10
4 free-range eggs
125 g (4½ oz) sugar
finely grated zest of 1 lemon
200 g (7 oz) cream cheese
400 ml (14 fl oz) double cream
200 g (7 oz) digestive biscuits, crushed
fresh figs, red currants or other
   berries, to decorate

1. Separate the yolks from the whites. Beat the yolks, sugar and zest in a bowl until fluffy, then mix in the cream cheese.
2. Whip the cream until fluffy and fold it into the mixture.
3. Whip the egg whites until stiff and carefully fold these into the mixture.
4. Layer the crushed biscuits with the mixture in a springform cake tin. Start and finish with layers of biscuit crumbs.
5. Tap the tin lightly against the table to disperse any air bubbles. Freeze the mixture for 3–4 hours, until it is slightly frozen.
6. Release the clip on the springform tin so that the cheesecake comes away freely. Serve it with figs, red currants or other berries.

cheesecake from Småland

MAKES 1 CHEESECAKE/SERVES 8–10
70 g (2½ oz) flour
2 litres (3½ pints) semi-skimmed milk
½ tbsp rennet
3 free-range eggs
3 tbsp sugar
200 ml (7 fl oz) double cream
100 g (4 oz) ground almonds
4 bitter almonds, finely grated
jam and lightly whipped cream,
   to serve

1. Whisk together the flour and 300 ml (10 fl oz) of the milk until smooth. Warm the rest of the milk until lukewarm.
2. Mix the flour mixture and the rennet into the lukewarm milk. Cover and leave to coagulate for about 30 minutes.
3. Pour the mixture through a fine sieve and let it drain for at least 4 hours but preferably overnight. Stir occasionally.
4. Preheat the oven to 175°C (350°F/gas 4).
5. Beat the eggs, sugar and cream together. Add the ground almonds and grated bitter almonds. Combine this mixture into the firm milk mixture.
6. Fill a buttered mould (about 15 x 20 cm/6 x 8 in) with the combined mixture.
7. Bake in the lower part of the oven for around 1 hour. Cover the cake with foil when it has turned golden, so it doesn't get too dark. Serve warm with jam and whipped cream.

say cheesecake!

bittersweet chocolate cheesecake

This is one for the real chocolate-lover. Chocolate cheesecake is the perfect luxury dessert – for a contrast of flavours serve it with some fresh raspberries. I usually make the base with Oreo or Maryland biscuits, but it is also good with ginger biscuits – just replace half of the digestive biscuits. If you replace all of the digestives the base can get too hard. The amount of time you bake the base remains the same.

MAKES 1 CHEESECAKE/SERVES 8–10

BISCUIT BASE
200 g (7 oz) digestive biscuits, crushed
200 g (7 oz) Maryland biscuits, crushed
2 tbsp good quality cocoa
125 g (4½ oz) butter

FILLING
500 g (18 oz) cream cheese
100 g (4 oz) sugar
1 vanilla pod, seeds scraped out
3 free-range eggs
200 g (7 oz) good quality dark
    chocolate, 70% cocoa solids
150 ml (5 fl oz) double cream
1½ tbsp rum
a handful of walnut halves

1. Preheat the oven to 175°C (350°F/gas 4).
2. Mix the crushed biscuit crumbs with the cocoa.
3. Melt the butter and mix it with the crumbs, then press into the base of a springform cake tin (24 cm/9½ in diameter).
4. Bake the base in the middle of the oven for about 7 minutes and let cool. Lower the oven temperature to 130°C (250°F/gas ½).
5. Beat together the cream cheese, sugar and seeds from a vanilla pod in a bowl until creamy.
6. Mix in one egg at a time.
7. Break the chocolate into pieces and melt in a bowl over a pan of boiling water (making sure the bowl doesn't touch the surface of the water).
8. Mix the melted chocolate, cream and rum into the mixture. Pour it over the base and garnish with whole walnuts.
9. Bake the cake for 40 minutes. Leave to cool and serve warm or at refrigerator temperature.

When I was in Italy for the first time, I found an enormous fig tree filled with sun-ripened figs while I was out walking in the countryside. It was an experience I'll never forget. I could just reach up and pick the large, juicy figs, which tasted sweet, fruity and completely fantastic. It is important to use good ingredients when you bake and cook. The flavour, after all, is in the ingredients. Don't bother with tasteless and unripe figs. If I can't find good produce – for example, if something is out of season – I'd rather make a different recipe for which good ingredients are currently available.

mascarpone cheesecake with figs

Mascarpone is a creamy Italian dessert cheese, and is widely available these days. This cheesecake is fantastically tasty and simple to make. It looks especially attractive if you make it in a fluted tin, but any loose-bottomed tin will do. You can replace the figs with another fruit or berry if figs are not in season.

MAKES 1 CHEESECAKE/SERVES 8–10

BISCUIT BASE

200 g (7 oz) digestive biscuits, crushed
100 g (4 oz) ginger biscuits, crushed
125 g (4½ oz) butter

FILLING

500 g (18 oz) mascarpone cheese
250 ml (9 fl oz) quark
100 g (4 oz) sugar
25 g (1 oz) corn flour
100 ml (3½ fl oz) double cream
1 vanilla pod, seeds scraped out
finely grated zest of 1 lime
3 free-range eggs

TOPPING

400 ml (14 fl oz) crème fraiche
12 fresh figs or berries, to garnish

1. Preheat the oven to 180°C (350°F/gas 4).
2. Melt the butter and mix it with the crumbs.
3. Press the crumb mixture into the bottom of a fluted loose-bottomed tin (26 cm/10½ inch diameter).
4. Prebake the base in the middle of the oven for about 10 minutes and let cool.
5. Whip the mascarpone and quark in a bowl until creamy.
6. Mix in the sugar, corn flour, cream, vanilla seeds and grated lime zest.
7. Mix in two eggs. Separate the third egg and only add the yolk to the mixture.
8. Pour the mixture over the base and bake the cake until golden in the lower part of the oven for around 1 hour.
9. Turn off the oven and leave the cake to stand in the oven for another 30 minutes.
10. Let the cake cool and chill until it is refrigerator temperature.
11. Whip the crème fraiche loosely with an electric mixer (just as you would double cream). Spread it over the cold cake and garnish with fresh figs or berries.

chocolate swirl cheesecake

For this cake, use chocolate with cocoa solids of less than 60 percent or else it will be too bitter. The flavour is wonderfully chocolatey without being too sweet.

MAKES 1 CHEESECAKE/SERVES 8–10

BISCUIT BASE

400 g (14 oz) digestive biscuits,
    crushed
150 g (5 oz) butter

FILLING

600 g (1 lb 5 oz) cream cheese
50 ml (2 fl oz) quark
125 g (4 1/2 oz) sugar
2 tsp vanilla sugar
4 free-range eggs
100 ml (3 1/2 fl oz) double cream

CHOCOLATE SWIRL

150 g (5 oz) good quality dark
    chocolate, 60% cocoa solids
3 tbsp espresso

1. Preheat the oven to 180°C (350°F/gas 4).
2. Melt the butter and mix it with the crushed biscuit crumbs.
3. Press the crumb mixture into the bottom of a loose-based cake tin (about 24 cm/9 1/2 in diameter).
4. Prebake the base in the middle of the oven for about 10 minutes and let cool. Lower the temperature of the oven to 130°C (250°F/gas 1/2).
5. Beat the cream cheese and quark in a bowl until creamy.
6. Mix in the sugar and vanilla sugar, then mix in one egg at a time followed by the cream.
7. Break the chocolate into pieces, melt it in a bowl over a pan of boiling water (making sure that the bowl does not touch the surface of the water) and mix in the coffee.
8. Mix half the cheesecake mixture with the chocolate.
9. Pour half of the remaining cheesecake mixture over the cake base.
10. Spoon half of the dark chocolate mixture over it, cover with the rest of the light mixture, then spoon the rest of the dark one on top.
11. Create a pattern in the combined mixture with the tip of a knife or toothpick.
12. Bake the cake for 1 hour and 25 minutes, until it is completely firm.
13. Let cool and serve the cake lukewarm or refrigerator-cold.

sweet potato cheesecake

Sweet potatoes are an under-appreciated root vegetable that work wonderfully in both savoury and sweet dishes. The flavour is complemented extremely well by cinnamon and ginger, so this cheesecake is perfect for Halloween or Christmas.

MAKES 1 CHEESECAKE/SERVES 8–10

BISCUIT BASE

150 g (5 oz) digestive biscuits, crushed
150 g (5 oz) ginger biscuits, crushed
125 g (4½ oz) butter

FILLING

1 large sweet potato (to make
    250 ml/9 fl oz) sweet potato purée)
600 g (1 lb 5 oz) cream cheese
125 g (4½ oz) butter
125 g (4½ oz) sugar
30 g (1½ oz) light muscovado sugar
1 tsp vanilla sugar
1 tsp ground cinnamon
1 tsp ground ginger
4 free-range eggs
3 tbsp double cream

1. Preheat the oven to 180°C (350°F/gas 4).
2. Melt the butter and mix it with the crumbs.
3. Press the crumb mixture into the bottom of a loose-based tin (about 24 cm/9½ in diameter).
4. Prebake the base in the middle of the oven for about 10 minutes.
5. In the meantime, peel and cube the sweet potato. Boil in lightly salted water until soft, about 20 minutes. Drain and mash or blend into a purée. You need 250 ml (9 fl oz) for this recipe. Let cool.
6. Beat the cream cheese and softened butter until creamy. Add the sugar and muscovado sugar.
7. Mix in the sweet potato purée, vanilla sugar, cinnamon and ginger, and stir until completely smooth.
8. Mix in one egg at a time, and then add the cream.
9. Pour the mixture over the base and bake in the lower part of the oven for 50–60 minutes. Shake the form lightly to see if the cake is ready; the mixture should be firm in the middle.
10. Turn off the oven and leave the cake to stand for another 30 minutes.

I like to take food to the beach since everything seems to taste better out in the fresh air. Cheesecake is perfect for a picnic because it's easily transportable and it isn't too delicate, and best of all it can be made in so many variations. It can be baked or frozen, and flavoured in so many different ways with various ingredients and cheeses. Of course, the baked kind is the one you want in your picnic basket.

new york cheesecake seven ways

This delicious cheesecake is baked in the traditional New York style – you'll find it in coffee shops and diners all over the Big Apple. It should be golden on top and impressively tall because it contains a lot of eggs. You can bake the cake in a large mould or in several small ones – it also looks good made in fluted tart tins or mini serving-sized moulds. But always use a springform tin for a large cheesecake.

BASIC RECIPE

MAKES 1 CHEESECAKE/SERVES 8–10

BISCUIT BASE

300 g (10 oz) digestive biscuits, crushed

150 g (5 oz) butter

FILLING

600 g (1 lb 5 oz)cream cheese

250 ml (9 fl oz) quark

100 g (4 oz) sugar

50 g (2 oz) corn flour

2 tsp vanilla sugar

3 free-range eggs

100 ml (3½ fl oz) double cream

200 g (7 oz) good quality white chocolate

1. Preheat the oven to 180°C (350°F/gas 4).
2. Melt the butter and mix it with the biscuit crumbs.
3. Press the crumb mixture into the bottom of a springform tin (about 24 cm/9½ in diameter).
4. Prebake the base in the middle of the oven for about 10 minutes and let cool.
5. Beat the cream cheese and quark until creamy.
6. Mix in the sugar, corn flour and vanilla sugar.
7. Mix in one egg at a time, then add the cream.
8. Break the chocolate into pieces, melt in a bowl over a pan of boiling water (don't allow the base of the bowl to touch the water). Blend the warm chocolate into the mixture.
9. Pour the mixture over the biscuit crumb base.
10. Bake the cheesecake in the middle of the oven for about 40 minutes. If needed, cover it with foil once it has turned golden to prevent it getting too dark.
11. Turn off the oven and leave the cake to stand for another 30 minutes.

lime cheesecake

MAKES 1 CHEESECAKE/SERVES 8–10

1 portion New York cheesecake (see basic recipe above)

finely grated zest of 5 limes, and the juice of 2 limes

1. Preheat the oven to 180°C (350°F/gas 4).
2. Make New York cheesecake according to the basic recipe and add the lime zest and juice to the mixture.
3. Pour the mixture over the biscuit base.
4. Bake the cheesecake in the middle of the oven for about 40 minutes.
5. Turn off the oven and leave the cake for another 30 minutes.

strawberry cheesecake

This is a real summer cake and is a big favourite with children. It looks great garnished with fresh strawberries. If you make it in several smaller tins with the biscuit base up the sides, you'll need to double the amount of biscuit base in the basic recipe, so there is enough for all the tins. If you want to make one big cake, this isn't necessary.

MAKES 1 CHEESECAKE/SERVES 8–10

1 portion New York cheesecake (see basic recipe page 48)
450 g (1 lb) fresh strawberries, sliced
2 tbsp sugar

1. Preheat the oven to 180°C (350°F/gas 4).
2. Make New York cheesecake according to the basic recipe.
3. Slice the strawberries and mash them with the sugar.
4. Strain away the juice and blend the strawberries into the mixture.
5. Pour the mixture over the biscuit base.
6. Bake the cheesecake in the middle of the oven for about 40 minutes the same as the basic recipe.
7. Turn off the oven and leave the cake for another 30 minutes.

pumpkin cheesecake

Pumpkin purée is sometimes hard to find, but it is easy to make your own. It takes a little time, but is worth the effort. Remember that the pumpkin's shell weighs a lot. For this recipe, you will need 450 g (1 lb) pumpkin without shell and seeds.

MAKES 1 CHEESECAKE/SERVES 8–10

1 portion New York cheesecake (see basic recipe page 48)
450 g (1 lb) pumpkin, peeled and deseeded (to replace the cream)
150 g (5 oz) ginger biscuits, crushed (to replace 150 g (5 oz) of digestives)
1 vanilla pod, seeds scraped out (instead of vanilla sugar)
1 pinch ground nutmeg
1½ tsp ground ginger
1 tsp ground cinnamon

1. Preheat the oven to 180°C (350°F/gas 4).
2. Cut the peeled and deseeded pumpkin into smaller pieces. Boil in water until soft, for 30-40 minutes. Drain well and cool. Process into a smooth purée and drain off any excess liquid. You need about 150 ml (5 fl oz) of thick purée.
3. Make the biscuit base according to the basic recipe, but replace half the digestives with crushed ginger biscuits. Prebake the base and let cool.
4. Make the cheesecake mixture according to the basic recipe, but replace the cream with the pumpkin and the vanilla sugar with vanilla seeds from the pod. Add the pumpkin purée, nutmeg, ginger and cinnamon, and pour the mixture over the biscuit base.
5. Bake the cheesecake in the middle of the oven for about 55 minutes, according to the basic recipe.
6. Turn off the oven and leave the cake to stand for another 30 minutes.

forest berry cheesecake

I usually bake this lovely cake with the biscuit mixture pushed up the sides a bit. If you want to try this, use a little extra butter and digestive biscuits.

MAKES 1 CHEESECAKE/SERVES 8–10

1 portion New York cheesecake
   (see basic recipe page 48)
100 g (4 oz) extra digestive biscuits,
   crushed
50 g (2 oz) extra butter
150 g (5 oz) fresh or frozen mixed
   berries

1. Preheat the oven to 180°C (350°F/gas 4).
2. Make the biscuit base according to the basic recipe, but add extra biscuits and butter and press the biscuit mixture up the sides of the tin. Make the cheesecake mixture according to the basic recipe.
3. Layer the mixture and berries over the biscuit base, finishing with berries on the top.
4. Bake the cheesecake in the middle of the oven for about 40 minutes, according to the basic recipe.
5. Turn off the oven and leave the cake to stand for another 30 minutes.

ricotta cheesecake

Ricotta, lemon and bitter almond make a totally wonderful flavour combination. This cheesecake is reminiscent of the Italian classic *torta della nonna* and is simply delicious – it also looks really nice made in a fluted loose-based tart tin. Decorate with a little icing sugar before serving.

MAKES 1 CHEESECAKE/SERVES 8-10

1 portion New York cheesecake
    (see basic recipe page 48)
500 g (18 oz) ricotta (instead of cream
    cheese)
100 ml (3½ oz) double cream
finely grated zest of 3 lemons
1 bitter almond, finely grated
50 g (2 oz) pine nuts
icing sugar, to decorate

1. Preheat the oven to 180°C (350°F/gas 4).
2. Make cheesecake according to the basic recipe, but replace the cream cheese with ricotta. Add an extra 100 ml (3½ oz) of cream and flavour the mixture with lemon zest and finely grated bitter almond. Make the biscuit base and put in a fluted loose-based tart tin, pressing it against the edges.
3. Pour the cream cheese mixture over the biscuit base. Sprinkle the pine nuts on top.
4. Bake the cheesecake in the middle of the oven for about 55 minutes. If needed, cover it with foil when it has turned golden so it doesn't get too dark.
5. Turn off the oven and leave the cake to stand for another 30 minutes. Dust with incing sugar to serve.

passion cheesecake

This variation of cheesecake with its fresh passion fruit taste is definitely my favourite. It is important to choose fruits with really wrinkled outer shells indicating ripeness in order to get the best results.

MAKES 1 CHEESECAKE/SERVES 8-10

1 portion New York cheesecake
    (see basic recipe page 48)
juice from 15 very ripe passion fruits
    (to replace the cream)
passion fruit, to decorate

1. Preheat the oven to 180°C (350°F/gas 4).
2. Cut open the passion fruits and scrape out the seeds and pulp. Strain and keep the juice. You need 150 ml (5 fl oz) passion fruit juice.
3. Make the cheesecake according to the basic recipe, but leave out the vanilla sugar and replace the cream with the passion fruit juice.
4. Pour the cheesecake mixture over the biscuit base.
5. Bake in the middle of the oven for about 50 minutes. If needed, cover it with aluminium foil when it has turned golden so it doesn't get too dark.
6. Turn off the oven and leave the cake to stand for another 30 minutes.

pancakes and waffles

There are few things that I long for as much as pancakes and waffles. And there are so many variations that it is actually impossible to get tired of them. If you want to appeal to both adults and kids when serving brunch, a snack or dinner, just warm up the griddle and get out the waffle iron. Here are the world's tastiest waffles and pancakes.

five variations on classic waffles

In Sweden we have eaten waffles since the 17th century and these days people eat the most waffles on Waffle Day, 25 March. This is because it is the Annunciation of the Virgin Mary, which was previously called 'the day of our lady' and has became Waffle Day due to the similarity in pronunciation in Swedish.

BASIC RECIPE
MAKES 10–12 WAFFLES
350 g (12 oz) plain flour
1½ tsp salt
2 tsp baking powder
800 ml (28 fl oz) milk
75 g (3 oz) butter
4 free-range eggs
melted butter for cooking

1. Mix the flour, salt, baking powder and half of the milk into a smooth batter.
2. Melt the butter, pour in the rest of the milk and beat it into the batter. Add the eggs.
3. Let the batter sit and expand for 20–30 minutes.
4. Warm the waffle iron, brush with melted butter and cook the waffles until golden.

lemon waffles

MAKES 10–12 WAFFLES
1 portion classic waffle batter
    (see basic recipe above)
finely grated zest of 2 lemons
melted butter for cooking

1. Make the waffle batter according to the basic recipe and add grated lemon zest to it.
2. Let the batter sit and expand for 20–30 minutes.
3. Warm the waffle iron, brush it with melted butter and cook the waffles until golden.

cardamom waffles

MAKES 10–12 WAFFLES
1 portion classic waffle batter (see basic recipe above)
½ tsp cardamom seeds
melted butter for cooking

1. Make the waffle batter according to the basic recipe.
2. Pound the cardamom seeds in a mortar until finely ground and add to the batter.
3. Let the batter sit and expand for 20–30 minutes.
4. Warm the waffle iron, brush it with melted butter and cook the waffles until golden.

blueberry waffles

MAKES 10–12 WAFFLES
1 portion classic waffle batter
   (see basic recipe page 62)
150 g (5 oz) fresh or frozen blueberries
melted butter for cooking

1. Make the waffle batter according to the basic recipe.
2. Let the batter sit and expand for 20–30 minutes.
3. Carefully fold the blueberries into the batter just before you begin cooking.
4. Warm the waffle iron, brush it with melted butter and cook the waffles until golden.

saffron waffles

MAKES 10–12 WAFFLES
1 portion classic waffle batter
   (see basic recipe page 62)
2 sachets (1 g) saffron threads
melted butter for cooking

1. Make the waffle batter according to the basic recipe, but warm the saffron together with the milk and let it cool before you blend it with the rest of the ingredients.
2. Let the batter sit and expand for 20–30 minutes.
3. Warm the waffle iron, brush it with melted butter and cook the waffles until golden.

world's tastiest crispy waffles

Not only are these crispy waffles delicious with whipped cream and jam, if you let them cool, you can then dip them in melted dark chocolate. Serve with blackberry jam or blueberry jam and lightly whipped cream.

MAKES 10 WAFFLES
275 ml (9½ oz) cold water
200 g (7 oz) plain flour
1 pinch sea salt
400 ml (14 fl oz) double cream
melted butter for cooking

1. Whisk the water, flour and salt into a smooth batter.
2. Whip the cream and carefully fold it into the mixture just before cooking.
3. Warm the waffle iron, brush it with melted butter and cook the waffles until golden.
4. Serve immediately so they retain their crispiness or let them cool by laying out on a cooling rack.

french toast

MAKES 12 SLICES/SERVES 6
6 free-range eggs
75 g (3 oz) plain flour
200 ml (7 fl oz) double cream
finely grated zest of 2 oranges
12 slices white bread
butter for frying
demerara sugar, vanilla ice cream and
    berries, to serve

1. Whisk the eggs and flour into a smooth batter in a mixing bowl.
2. Mix in the cream and grated orange zest.
3. Dip the bread slices into the mixture so that they absorb the liquid.
4. Fry the dipped slices of bread in butter until golden in a frying pan over medium heat.
5. Dip the newly fried slices of bread in demerara sugar and serve warm with vanilla ice cream and berries.

poor knights

MAKES 8 SLICES/SERVES 4
1 portion classic pancake batter
    (see basic recipe page 68)
8 slices white bread
2½ tbsp ground cinnamon
200 g (7 oz) sugar
butter for frying
jam and lightly whipped cream to serve

1. Make the pancake batter according to the basic recipe.
2. Dip the bread slices so they absorb the liquid.
3. Fry the dipped slices of bread in butter until golden in a frying pan over medium heat.
4. Mix the cinnamon and sugar in a deep plate and dip the newly fried slices of bread in the sugar, then serve warm with jam and lightly whipped cream.

seven variations on belgian waffles

These wonderful waffles originally come from Brussels, where they are sold by street vendors. The waffles are often powdered with icing sugar and sometimes served with chocolate sauce and whipped cream. They are traditionally made in a Belgium waffle iron, which is large, thick and rectangular. I think they are perfect for brunch served with fruit and berries, powdered sugar, cream or a little softened vanilla ice cream.

BASIC RECIPE

MAKES 4 LARGE WAFFLES

2 free-range eggs
125 g (4½ oz) butter
250 ml (9 fl oz) semi-skimmed milk
200 ml (7 fl oz) water
12 g (⅓ oz) fresh yeast
½ tsp salt
75 g (3 oz) sugar
2 tsp vanilla sugar
450 g (1 lb) plain flour
melted butter for cooking

1. Separate the yolks from the whites (without getting any yolk in the whites).
2. Melt the butter, add milk and water and warm until the liquid is lukewarm.
3. Crumble the yeast in a bowl and dissolve it in the liquid.
4. Add the yolks, salt, sugar, vanilla sugar and flour, and mix into a smooth batter.
5. Whip the egg whites into soft peaks in a clean mixing bowl, then carefully fold them into the batter and let it rest for around 20 minutes.
6. Warm the waffle iron, brush it with melted butter and cook the waffles for 3–5 minutes.

belgian waffles with caramel and banana

MAKES 4 LARGE WAFFLES

1 portion batter for Belgian waffles (see basic recipe above)
1 small packet chocolate caramel sweets
2 ripe bananas
melted butter for cooking

1. Make the waffle batter according to the basic recipe.
2. Thinly slice the caramels and bananas and fold them into the batter.
3. Warm the waffle iron, brush it with melted butter and cook the waffles for 3–5 minutes.

coconut belgian waffles

MAKES 4 LARGE WAFFLES

1 portion batter for Belgian waffles (see basic recipe above)
50 g (2 oz) coconut flakes
melted butter for cooking

1. Make the waffle batter according to the basic recipe and add the coconut flakes.
2. Warm the waffle iron, brush it with melted butter and cook the waffles for 3–5 minutes.

strawberry belgian waffles

MAKES 4 LARGE WAFFLES

1 portion batter for Belgian waffles
   (see basic recipe page 65)

300 g (10 oz) fresh strawberries

melted butter for cooking

1. Make the waffle batter according to the basic recipe.
2. Slice the strawberries into small pieces and mix them into the batter.
3. Warm the waffle iron, brush it with melted butter and cook the waffles for 3–5 minutes.

blueberry belgian waffles with lemon

MAKES 4 LARGE WAFFLES

1 portion batter for Belgian waffles
   (see basic recipe page 65)

finely grated zest of 4 lemons

75 g (3 oz) fresh or frozen blueberries

melted butter for cooking

1. Make the waffle batter according to the basic recipe.
2. Carefully fold the lemon zest and blueberries into the batter right before cooking.
3. Warm the waffle iron, brush it with melted butter and cook the waffles for 3–5 minutes.

chocolate belgian waffles

MAKES 4 LARGE WAFFLES

1 portion batter for Belgian waffles
   (see basic recipe page 65)

100 g (4 oz) good quality dark
   chocolate, 70% cocoa solids

2½ tbsp dark muscovado sugar

melted butter for cooking

1. Make the waffle batter according to the basic recipe.
2. Chop and melt the chocolate in a bowl over but not touching a pan of boiling water, then mix with the muscovado.
3. Mix the chocolate into the batter.
4. Warm the waffle iron, brush it with melted butter and cook the waffles for 3–5 minutes.

black and white belgian waffles

MAKES 4 LARGE WAFFLES

1 portion batter for Belgian waffles
   (see basic recipe page 65)

100 g (4 oz) good quality dark
   chocolate, 70% cocoa solids

150 g (5 oz) good quality white
   chocolate

melted butter for cooking

1. Make the waffle batter according to the basic recipe.
2. Melt the dark chocolate in a bowl over but not touching a pan of boiling water, then mix it into the batter.
3. Coarsely chop the white chocolate and fold it into the batter.
4. Warm the waffle iron, brush it with melted butter and cook the waffles for 3–5 minutes.

russian blinis

Blinis are a typical appetizer in Russia – these fluffy, puffy and tasty buckwheat pancakes are traditionally served with smetana (a type of crème fraiche) and Russian caviar. I serve them with whitefish roe, crème fraiche, finely chopped red onion, dill and lemon. Fry the blinis in a small pan for the most beautiful results and don't be stingy with the batter. These blinis should be really fluffy.

MAKES 6 BLINIS
2 free-range eggs
200 ml (7 fl oz) milk
12 g (⅓ oz) fresh yeast
100 ml (3½ fl oz) lager
125 g (4½ oz) buckwheat flour
75 g (3 oz) plain flour
1 tsp salt
50 g (2 oz) butter
butter for cooking
whitefish roe, crème fraiche, finely chopped red onion, dill and lemon, to serve

1. Separate the yolks from the whites.
2. Warm the milk until it is lukewarm.
3. Crumble the yeast in a bowl, stir in the milk and lager and mix until the yeast is dissolved.
4. Whisk the flours in a little at a time and add salt and yolks.
5. Let the batter rise in the bowl under a cloth until it doubles in size, about an hour.
6. Melt the butter, let it cool and mix it into the batter.
7. Whip the egg whites into stiff peaks and carefully fold them into the batter.
8. Cook the blinis in butter into small, thick pancakes (10 cm/4 inches in diameter) in a pan over medium heat.
9. Serve with whitefish roe, crème fraiche, finely chopped red onion, dill and lemon.

classic swedish pancakes

Pancakes have been made and eaten in Sweden for a long time, with many local variations. One traditional dessert is pancakes served with jam and cream, after pea soup on Thursday night. Our pancakes never seem old-fashioned and I think they are just as good any day of the week. And of course children love them.

BASIC RECIPE
MAKES 10 PANCAKES
275 g (13 oz) plain flour
½ tsp salt
1½ tsp sugar
800 ml (28 fl oz) milk
1 tbsp butter
2 free-range eggs
butter for cooking

1. Mix the flour, salt, sugar and half of the milk into a smooth batter.
2. Melt the butter, pour in the rest of the milk and whisk it into the batter. Add the eggs.
3. Let the better stand for 20–30 minutes.
4. Melt a knob of butter in a frying pan over medium heat and cook thin pancakes. Turn them over when they have stiffened slightly and the underside has turned golden.

seven variations on ricotta pancakes

Ricotta is an Italian cream cheese that should be consumed as fresh as possible. Many Italians only eat it on the day it is made. It has a slightly grainy, soft consistency with a fresh, mild taste that makes it perfect for these delicious pancakes

BASIC RECIPE

MAKES 8 PANCAKES

3 free-range eggs

250 g (9 oz) ricotta

250 ml (9 fl oz) semi-skimmed milk

175 g (6 oz) plain flour

1 tsp baking powder

1 pinch salt

butter for cooking

maple syrup, fresh berries and vanilla
   ice cream, to serve

1. Separate the egg yolks from the whites.
2. Mix the ricotta, milk and yolks in a mixing bowl.
3. Blend the flour, baking powder and salt and mix it into the batter.
4. Whip the egg whites until fluffy and carefully fold them into the batter.
5. Melt a knob of butter in a frying pan over medium heat. Spoon the batter into the pan (making 8 pancakes altogether). Cook until golden on both sides.
6. Serve with maple syrup, fresh berries and vanilla ice cream.

ricotta pancakes with blueberries

MAKES 8 PANCAKES

1 portion batter for ricotta pancakes
   (see basic recipe above)

150 g (5 oz) fresh or frozen blueberries

butter for cooking

maple syrup and vanilla ice cream,
   to serve

1. Make the batter according to the basic recipe and carefully fold the blueberries into the batter.
2. Melt a knob of butter in a frying pan over medium heat. Spoon the batter into the pan. Cook the pancakes until golden on both sides.
3. Serve with maple syrup and vanilla ice cream.

ricotta pancakes with strawberries

MAKES 8 PANCAKES

1 portion batter for ricotta pancakes
   (see basic recipe above)

175 g (6 oz) fresh strawberries, sliced

butter for cooking

maple syrup and vanilla ice cream,
   to serve

1. Make the batter according to the basic recipe, then fold the sliced stawberries into the batter.
2. Melt a knob of butter in a frying pan over medium heat. Spoon the batter into the pan. Cook until golden on both sides to make 8 pancakes.
3. Serve with maple syrup and vanilla ice cream.

ricotta pancakes with mixed berries

MAKES 8 PANCAKES

1 portion batter for ricotta pancakes
   (see basic recipe page 71)
1 handful fresh strawberries, sliced
75 g (3 oz) fresh or frozen raspberries
75 g (3 oz) fresh or frozen blueberries
butter for cooking
maple syrup and vanilla ice cream, to
   serve

1. Make the batter according to the basic recipe, and carefully fold the sliced strawberries and other berries into the batter.
2. Melt a knob of butter in a frying pan over medium heat. Spoon the batter into the pan. Cook until golden on both sides to make 8 pancakes.
3. Serve with maple syrup and vanilla ice cream.

ricotta pancakes with banana

MAKES 8 PANCAKES

1 portion batter for ricotta pancakes
   (see basic recipe page 71)
3 ripe bananas, sliced
butter for cooking
maple syrup and vanilla ice cream, to
   serve

1. Make the batter according to the basic recipe and fold the sliced bananas into the batter.
2. Melt a knob of butter in a frying pan over medium heat. Spoon the batter into the pan to make 8 pancakes Cook until golden on both sides.
3. Serve with maple syrup and vanilla ice cream.

ricotta pancakes with chocolate and banana

MAKES 8 PANCAKES

1 portion batter for ricotta pancakes
   (see basic recipe page 71)
3 ripe bananas, sliced
200 g (7 oz) good quality dark
   chocolate, 70% cocoa solids
butter for cooking
maple syrup, vanilla ice cream to serve

1. Make the batter according to the basic recipe.
2. Coarsely chop the chocolate, and fold this and the sliced bananas into the batter.
3. Melt a knob of butter in a frying pan over medium heat. Spoon the batter into the pan to make 8 pancakes. Cook until golden on both sides.
4. Serve with maple syrup and vanilla ice cream.

ricotta pancakes with pecans and chocolate

MAKES 8 pancakes

1 portion batter for ricotta pancakes
   (see basic recipe page 71)
50 g (2 oz) pecans, chopped
200 g (7 oz) good quality dark
   chocolate, 70% cocoa solids
butter for cooking
maple syrup, vanilla ice cream to serve

1. Make the batter according to the basic recipe
2. Coarsely chop the chocolate and fold with the chopped pecans into the batter.
3. Melt a knob of butter in a frying pan over medium heat. Spoon the batter into the pan to make 8 pancakes. Cook until golden on both sides.
4. Serve with maple syrup and vanilla ice cream.

french crêpes

Crêpes are ubiquitous in France, filled with both sweet and savoury fillings. They are made thinner and larger than normal pancakes, but you can make them in a regular frying pan. I have many favourite recipe but probably the best is the classic Crêpes Suzette, which is crêpes with butter, sugar and the zest and juice from an orange flambéed in Cointreau. Another favourite is apples fried in butter with Calvados and vanilla ice cream.

MAKES 12–15 CRÊPES

200 g (7 oz) plain flour
1 pinch salt
1 tbsp sugar
1 tsp vanilla sugar
finely grated zest of 1 lemon
3 free-range eggs
660 ml (23 fl oz) milk
3 tbsp butter
butter for cooking
sugar and freshly grated zest of
    1 orange, to serve

1. Mix the flour, salt, sugar, vanilla sugar and lemon zest in a mixing bowl.
2. Add the eggs and a little milk at a time, and whisk until the batter is smooth.
3. Melt the butter and add it to the batter.
4. Let the batter sit for 15–20 minutes.
5. Melt a knob of butter in a frying pan over medium heat, smooth out the batter with a spatula and make really thin crêpes.
6. Once done fold them into half-moons and then fold once more. Serve with sugar and grated orange peel.

american pancakes

These pancakes are traditionally served for breakfast with maple syrup and a knob of butter. The Yankees also like to eat bacon with pancakes, but I think these are best with vanilla ice cream. You can also top with fresh berries or sliced bananas. If you are not going to eat them right away, keep them warm in the oven.

MAKES 8 PANCAKES
225 g (8 oz) plain flour
2 tsp baking powder
½ tsp salt
2 tbsp sugar
2 tsp vanilla sugar
finely grated zest of 1 lemon
2 tbsp butter
250 ml (9 fl oz) semi-skimmed milk
1 free-range egg
butter for cooking
icing sugar and vanilla ice cream,
    to serve

1. Mix the flour, baking powder, salt, sugar, vanilla sugar and grated lemon zest in a mixing bowl.
2. Melt the butter, whisk with the milk and the egg and mix this into the bowl with the dry ingredients.
3. Cook the pancakes in butter until golden in a frying pan over medium heat.
4. Serve warm with icing sugar and vanilla ice cream.

buttermilk pancakes

Classic buttermilk pancakes are served in diners all over the USA. They taste fantastic but are not quite as fluffy as American pancakes. This delicious dish is usually served with maple syrup and butter.

MAKES 10 PANCAKES
175 g (6 oz) plain flour
1 tsp bicarbonate of soda
½ tsp salt
50 g (2 oz) polenta
50 g (2 oz) sugar
1 tbsp butter
350 ml (12 fl oz) buttermilk
2 free-range eggs
butter for cooking
butter and maple syrup, to serve

1. Mix the dry ingredients in a mixing bowl.
2. Melt the butter and mix it with the buttermilk and eggs.
3. Mix the egg batter with the dry ingredients.
4. Cook the pancakes in butter until golden in a frying pan over medium heat.
5. Serve warm with butter and maple syrup.

saffron pancake

Here is my take on the saffron pancake from Gotland. It is a favourite at Christmas and is a perfect way to use up leftover rice pudding. If that is the case, you can skip the first step in the recipe – cooking the rice – and begin by boiling a little milk with saffron and mixing it into the pudding.

MAKES 1 DISH/8 SERVINGS

125 g (4½ oz) short-grain rice
150 ml (5 fl oz) water
500 ml (18 fl oz) semi-skimmed milk
½ tsp salt
2 sachets (1 g) saffron strands
6 free-range eggs
2 tbsp plain flour
200 g (7 oz) almond paste, grated
25 g (1 oz) flaked almonds
butter for the dish
jam and lightly whipped cream, to serve

1. Boil the rice and water in a pot with the lid on until the water has been absorbed. Add the milk and salt.
2. Boil the rice for about 30 minutes. Stir occasionally and add the saffron towards the end of the cooking time. Let the rice cool.
3. Preheat the oven to 180°C (350°F/gas 4).
4. Whisk the eggs in a bowl and add the flour, grated almond paste and the saffron infused rice mixture.
5. Pour the batter into a buttered, oven-safe dish and sprinkle with flaked almonds.
6. Bake the pancake in the middle of the oven for about 30 minutes, until it is golden and the batter is completely firm.
7. Serve the pancake with lightly whipped cream and jam.

cardamom pancake

MAKES 1 DISH/6 SERVINGS

1 tbsp butter
1 litre (1½ pts) semi-skimmed milk
100 g (4 oz) semolina
2 tsp cardamom seeds
3 free-range eggs
100 g (4 oz) sugar
75 g (3 oz) plain flour
1 tsp salt
butter for the dish
jam and lightly whipped cream, to serve

1. Preheat the oven to 180°C (350°F/gas 4).
2. Melt the butter in a large pan and add the milk.
3. When the milk is boiling, add the semolina, and cook it for about 5 minutes into porridge. Let it cool somewhat.
4. Finely grind the cardamom in a mortar.
5. Mix together the cardamom, eggs, sugar, flour and salt, and whisk it into the porridge.
6. Butter a dish and pour the pancake batter into it.
7. Bake the pancake until it is golden in the middle of the oven for about 45 minutes.
8. Let it cool and serve the pancake with jam and lightly whipped cream.

ciao tortano

Tortano is a filled round bread that comes from the Naples region in Italy. It is shaped like a ring and gets its name from its cake-like shape and because it is cut into cake-like slices. The original is filled with boiled eggs, but I fill my tortano breads with lots of other tasty things. It is perfect to take on an excursion or a picnic. Since it is filled with nice cheeses and cold meats such as ham and salami and also with vegetables, it makes a lovely light lunch. All you have to do is choose your favourite recipe.

nine kinds of tortano

Tortano is the perfect bread for the picnic basket or the buffet. It is unbelievably delicious and filling and also really easy to vary. You can make the bread in a flash and then just choose a filling from among your favourite ingredients.

BASIC RECIPE

MAKES 1 ROUND BREAD

15 g (½ oz) fresh yeast

300 ml (10 fl oz) lukewarm water

2 tbsp olive oil

1 tbsp honey

1½ tbsp sea salt

175 g (6 oz) durum wheat flour

275 g (9½ oz) strong bread flour

choice of filling (see variations)

1. Crumble the yeast in a mixing bowl and dissolve it in the water, olive oil, honey and sea salt.
2. Mix in the flours a little at a time; knead until the dough becomes elastic (about 10 minutes).
3. Let it rise in the bowl under a cloth, until it doubles in size, about 40 minutes.
4. Press the dough into a rectangle about 1 cm (½ inch) thick. Don't roll it, because the air will be pressed out of the dough.
5. Fill the dough with the filling of your choice (see variations).
6. Brush the edges of the dough with water and roll it into a long sausage shape, then shape into a wreath.
7. Preheat the oven to 250°C (500°F/gas 10).
8. Place on a tray lined with baking parchment, flour the bread and let it rise under a cloth for around 30 minutes.
9. Put the tray in the oven and lower the temperature to 200°C (400°F/gas 6). Bake for around 35 minutes and let it cool on a cooling rack.

tortano with prosciutto and mozzarella

MAKES 1 ROUND BREAD

1 portion tortano dough (see basic recipe above)

200 g (7 oz) mozzarella cheese

200 g (7 oz) prosciutto

1 bunch fresh basil

1. Make the tortano according to the basic recipe.
2. Slice the mozzarella and layer it over the dough together with the prosciutto and basil leaves.
3. Brush the edges of the dough with water and roll it into a long sausage shape, then shape into a wreath.
4. Preheat the oven to 250°C (500°F/gas 10).
5. Place on a tray lined with baking parchment, flour the bread and let it rise under a cloth for around 30 minutes.
6. Put the tray in the oven and lower the temperature to 200°C (400°F/gas 6). Bake for around 35 minutes and let it cool on a cooling rack.

tortano with goats' cheese, honey and walnuts

I take this tasty bread with me on a spring picnic or to a potluck supper. It is fantastic and tastes like delicious *chèvre chaud*, which is a wonderful toasted sandwich with goats' cheese, honey and walnuts.

MAKES 1 ROUND BREAD

1 portion tortano (see basic recipe page 82)

200 g chèvre or other similar goats' cheese

150 g (5 oz) walnuts, roughly chopped

2 tbsp honey, clear

1. Make the tortano according to the basic recipe.
2. Break the chèvre into pieces then layer the cheese and chopped walnuts over the dough. Drizzle with honey.
3. Brush the edges of the dough with water and roll it into a sausage shape. Shape it into a wreath.
4. Preheat the oven to 250°C (500°F/gas 10).
5. Place on a tray lined with baking parchment, flour the bread and let it rise under a cloth for around 30 minutes.
6. Put the tray in the oven and lower the temperature to 200°C (400°F/gas 6). Bake for around 35 minutes and then let it cool on a cooling rack.

tortano with feta and olives

Greek feta is a really good sharp cheese that I always have in my refrigerator. Since it is packed in its own brine, it lasts a long time. Buy imported feta from Greek companies, since these always have the best flavour.

MAKES 1 ROUND BREAD

1 portion tortano (see basic recipe page 82)

200 g (7 oz) feta cheese

5 g (2 oz) black olives, chopped

3 sprigs rosemary, leaves stripped and fincly chopped

2 tbsp fennel seeds

2 tbsp honey, clear

freshly ground black pepper

1. Make the tortano according to the basic recipe.
2. Crumble the feta. Lightly pound the fennel seeds in a mortar. Layer the ingredients over the dough. Drizzle with honey and season with pepper.
3. Brush the edges of the dough with water and roll it into a sausage shape. Shape it into a wreath.
4. Preheat the oven to 250°C (500°F/gas 10).
5. Place on a tray lined with baking parchment, flour the bread and let it rise under a cloth for around 30 minutes.
6. Put the tray in the oven and lower the temperature to 200°C (400°F/gas 6). Bake for around 35 minutes and then let it cool on a cooling rack.

tortano with roasted vegetables and feta

Inviting friends to a picnic or a garden party in the summer is one of the best things there is. I think that such events should be spontaneous and unpretentious. Tortano is the perfect food for such an occasion, simple and appealing to most people.

MAKES 1 ROUND BREAD

1 portion tortano (see basic recipe
    page 82)

200 g (7 oz) feta cheese

3 sprigs rosemary, leaves stripped and
    finely chopped

2 tbsp fennel seeds

1 carrot, peeled and diced

1 parsnip, peeled and diced

5 artichoke hearts, chopped

1 small onion, finely chopped

2 cloves garlic, thinly sliced

butter

sea salt

freshly ground black pepper

2 tbsp honey, clear

1. Crumble the feta cheese and lightly pound the fennel seeds in a mortar. Peel and dice the vegetables into small cubes.
2. Fry the vegetables and garlic in butter until soft and season with salt and pepper. Let cool.
3. Make the tortano according to the basic recipe.
4. Layer the feta with the vegetables, rosemary and fennel over the dough. Drizzle with honey.
5. Brush the edges of the dough with water and roll it into a sausage shape. Shape it into a wreath.
6. Preheat the oven to 250°C (500°F/gas 10).
7. Place on a tray lined with baking parchment, flour the bread and let it rise under a cloth for around 30 minutes.
8. Put the tray in the oven and lower the temperature to 200°C (400°F/gas 6). Bake the bread for around 35 minutes and let it cool on a cooling rack.

tortano with portobello mushrooms

Portobello is a type of mushroom that you can find in most shops and some supermarkets these days. I never wash any mushrooms, just carefully brush them off with a brush or peel the upper layer from the top with a little knife. You can also cut off most of the gills underneath the cap. I do this so that the Portobello mushroom has a more pleasant and firmer consistency when I fry it in butter.

MAKES 1 ROUND BREAD

1 portion tortano (see basic recipe
   page 82)
3 large portobello mushrooms, sliced
2 garlic cloves, finely sliced
2 tbsp butter
sea salt
freshly ground black pepper
250 g (9 oz) mozzarella cheese
3 sprigs rosemary, leaves stripped and
   finely chopped
200 g (7 oz) smoked ham

1. Fry the mushrooms and garlic in butter until soft and they have turned golden; season with salt and pepper. Let cool.
2. Make the tortano according to the basic recipe.
3. Slice the mozzarella then layer the mozzarella, mushrooms, rosemary and ham over the dough.
4. Brush the edges of the dough with water and roll it into a thick sausage shapel. Shape it into a wreath.
5. Preheat the oven to 250°C (500°F/gas 10).
6. Place the wreath on a tray lined with baking parchment, flour the bread and let it rise under a cloth for around 30 minutes.
7. Put the tray in the oven and lower the temperature to 200°C (400°F/gas 6). Bake the bread for around 35 minutes and let it cool on a cooling rack.

tortano with goats' cheese and salami

MAKES 1 ROUND BREAD

1 portion tortano (see basic recipe
   page 82)
125 g (4½ oz) mozzarella cheese
100 g (4 oz) chèvre or other similar
   goats' cheese
1 handful mixed olives, stoned and
   chopped
1 handful red cherry tomatoes, halved
3 sprigs rosemary, leaves stripped and
   finely chopped
200 g (7 oz) salami
freshly ground black pepper

1. Make the tortano according to the basic recipe.
2. Slice the mozzarella, crumble the chèvre, stone the olives, halve the tomatoes and finely chop the rosemary.
3. Layer all the ingredients over the dough.
4. Brush the edges of the dough with water and roll it into a thick sausage shape. Shape it into a wreath.
5. Preheat the oven to 250°C (500°F/gas 10).
6. Place the wreath on a tray lined with baking parchment, flour the bread and let it rise under a cloth for around 30 minutes.
7. Put the tray in the oven and lower the temperature to 200°C (400°F/gas 6). Bake the bread for around 35 minutes and let it cool on a cooling rack.

tomato tortano

I bake this beautiful red bread with sun-dried tomatoes. Choose sun-dried tomatoes in oil and drain them before using in this recipe bread. Use the flavoured oil from the tomatoes in the dough instead of ordinary olive oil.

MAKES 1 ROUND BREAD

1 portion tortano (see basic recipe
   page 82)
2 tbsp oil from sun-dried tomatoes
25 g (1 oz) strong bread flour
20 sun-dried tomatoes
250 g (8 oz) mozzarella cheese
1 bunch oregano, leaves stripped

1. Make the tortano according to the basic recipe, but replace the olive oil with the oil from the sun-dried tomatoes and add an extra 25 g (1 oz) flour. Finely chop half of the sun-dried tomatoes and mix them into the dough.
2. Shred the rest of the sun-dried tomatoes and layer them over the dough with the sliced mozzarella cheese and the oregano leaves.
3. Brush the edges of the dough with water and roll it into a thick sausage shape. Shape it into a wreath.
4. Preheat the oven to 250°C (500°F/gas 10).
5. Place the wreath on a tray lined with baking parchment, flour the bread, cover and let it rise for around 30 minutes.
6. Put the tray in the oven and lower the temperature to 200°C (400°F/gas 6). Bake the bread for around 35 minutes and let it cool on a cooling rack.

tortano quattro formaggi

This is the bread for real cheese-lovers. If you can't find the Italian cheese Fontina, you can replace it with some other matured hard cheese. You can always choose your own favourite cheeses.

1 BREAD

1 portion tortano (see basic recipe
   page 82)
350 g (12 oz) mixed cheeses
   (Parmesan, Fontina, Taleggio and
   Gorgonzola)

1. Make the tortano according to the basic recipe.
2. Grate the Parmesan and Fontina cheeses and crumble the Taleggio and Gorgonzola cheeses. Distribute the cheeses over the dough.
3. Brush the edges of the dough with water and roll it into athick sausage shape. Shape it into a wreath.
4. Preheat the oven to 250°C (500°F/gas 10).
5. Place the wreath on a tray lined with baking parchment, flour the bread, cover and let it rise for around 30 minutes.
6. Put the tray in the oven and lower the temperature to 200°C (400°F/gas 6). Bake the bread for around 35 minutes and let it cool on a cooling rack.

brownies and blondies

Brownies are the American answer to chocolate cake bars. I think they should be compact and sticky and never dry and crumbly. They can be decorated with icing and, as you will see in this chapter, brownies can be flavoured in many different ways. Blondies are the fair cousin to brownies and they get their caramel flavour from brown sugar and white chocolate.

nine variations on brownies

I learned this fantastic basic recipe for American brownies when I worked at a French bakery. Like all the best baking it contains good quality ingredients – free-range eggs, good cocoa powder and fresh dairy products – to make a simple but delicious chocolate treat. This basic brownie recipe can be varied in tons of different ways.

BASIC RECIPE
MAKES 24 SQUARES
350 g (12 oz) softened butter
500 g (18 oz) sugar
150 g (5 oz) good quality cocoa powder
100 ml (3½ fl oz) golden syrup
½ tsp salt
6 free-range eggs
200 g (7 oz) plain flour

CHOCOLATE ICING
125 g (4 oz) softened butter
550 g (1 lb 4 oz) icing sugar
75 g (3 oz) good quality cocoa powder
2 tsp vanilla sugar
200 g (7 oz) cream cheese
1 tbsp warm coffee

1. Preheat the oven to 180°C (350°F/gas 6.
2. Cream the butter and sugar until white and creamy.
3. Add the cocoa, syrup and salt.
4. Mix in the eggs, one at a time. Add the flour to the batter last.
5. Place baking parchment on the bottom of a baking tin and fill the dish with the batter.
6. Bake the cake in the middle of the oven for 30–35 minutes. Put a toothpick or knife in the middle; the cake should be a little sticky. Let it cool.

For the icing:
1. Beat together the butter, icing sugar, cocoa and vanilla sugar until creamy.
2. Add the cream cheese and coffee and whisk into a smooth frosting. Spread over the brownies.

after eight brownies

I love the combination of chocolate and mint so for me this is the ultimate brownie.
I like to serve these with some lightly whipped cream.

MAKES 24 SQUARES
1 portion brownie batter (see basic recipe, page 96)
200 g (7 oz) After Eight chocolates

1. Make the brownie batter according to the basic recipe.
2. Place baking parchment on the bottom of a baking tin and fill the dish with the batter.
3. Put whole After Eight chocolates in the middle of the batter (so they are covered with batter).
4. Bake in the middle of the oven for 30–35 minutes. Check for doneness with a toothpick; it should be a little sticky.
5. Let it cool and then slice it into squares.

raspberry brownies

MAKES 24 SQUARES
1 portion brownie batter (see basic
  recipe page 96)
300 g (10 oz) fresh or frozen
  raspberries

1. Make the brownie batter according to the basic recipe and
   carefully fold the raspberries into it.
2. Place baking parchment on the bottom of a baking tin and fill
   the dish with the batter.
3. Bake in the middle of the oven for 30-35 minutes. Use a
   toothpick to test for doneness; it should be a little sticky.
4. Let it cool and then slice the brownies into squares.

lemon brownies with blackberries

MAKES 24 SQUARES
1 portion brownie batter (see basic
  recipe page 96)
finely grated zest of 6 lemons
300 g (10 oz) fresh or frozen
  blackberries

1. Make the brownie batter according to the basic recipe, then
   add grated lemon zest and fold the berries into the batter.
2. Place baking parchment on the bottom of a baking tin and
   fill the dish with the batter.
3. Bake in the middle of the oven for 30-35 minutes. Test for
   doneness with a toothpick; the cake should be a little sticky.
4. Let it cool and then slice into squares.

double hazelnut brownies

I'm a real Nutella freak. I know that it's a little childish, but it is a very useful spread
that tastes of hazelnut and can be bought in a jar. I use it in everything from crêpes to
semifreddo. It's fantastic in these brownies.

MAKES 24 SQUARES
1 portion brownie batter (see basic
  recipe page 96)
300 g (10 oz) hazelnuts
350 g (10 oz) Nutella, at room
  temperature

1. Make the brownie batter according to the basic recipe.
2. Roast the hazelnuts in a hot frying pan, place them in a towel
   and rub away most of the skin.
3. Fold the nuts into the batter.
4. Place baking parchment on the bottom of a baking tin and fill
   the dish with the batter.
5. Spoon or drizzle the Nutella over the batter and draw a
   pattern through the Nutella with a knife, so the cake looks
   marbled.
6. Bake in the middle of the oven for 30-35 minutes. Test for
   doneness with a toothpick; the cake should be a little sticky.
7. Let it cool and then slice into squares.

lavender brownies

Chocolate and lavender are flavours that get on well together. The taste is flowery and a little spicy. In this recipe, you can use both fresh and dried flowers. If you use dried lavender, you need less because the flavour is more concentrated.

MAKES 24 SQUARES

1 portion brownie batter (see basic
    recipe page 96)
2 tbsp fresh lavender, crushed
400 g (14 oz) good quality dark
    chocolate, 70% cocoa solids

FUDGE ICING

300 ml (10 fl oz) double cream
100 ml (3½ fl oz) milk
100 ml (3½ fl oz) golden syrup
400 g (14 oz) good quality dark
    chocolate, 70% cocoa solids
fresh lavender and lightly whipped
    cream to serve

1. Make the brownie batter according to the basic recipe and add the lavender.
2. Coarsely chop the chocolate and mix it into the batter.
3. Place baking parchment on the bottom of a baking tin and fill the dish with the batter.
4. Bake in the middle of the oven for 30–35 minutes. Test for doneness with a toothpick; the cake should be alittle sticky.

ICING

1. Boil the cream, milk and syrup. Remove the pot from the heat and let the liquid cool a few degrees.
2. Finely chop the chocolate and fold it into the warm cream so the chocolate melts.
3. Spread the icing over the cake and refrigerate until the icing is firm.
4. Slice the cake into squares and serve with lightly whipped cream and fresh lavender flowers.

chunky monkey brownies

Chunky monkey is a flavour of ice cream from Ben and Jerry's that contains chocolate, banana and walnuts. Those flavours work really well in brownies. Serve vanilla ice cream with this for a really delicious dessert.

MAKES 24 SQUARES

1 portion brownie batter (see basic
    recipe page 96)
3 ripe bananas, sliced
300 g (10 oz) good quality dark
    chocolate, 70% cocoa solids
200 g (7 oz) walnuts, chopped

1. Make the brownie batter according to the basic recipe.
2. Coarsely chop the chocolate, then fold it and the bananas and walnuts into the batter.
3. Place baking parchment on the bottom of a baking tin and fill the dish with the batter.
4. Bake the cake in the middle of the oven for 30–35 minutes. Test for doneness with a toothpick; the cake should still be a little sticky.
5. Let it cool and then slice the brownies into squares.

rocky road brownies

Rocky Road is a classic American sweet that became a star when I made it on one of my programmes. Since it is so good, I had to use the flavours again in this tasty little treat.

MAKES 24
1 portion brownie batter (see basic
   recipe page 96)

FUDGE ICING
300 ml (10 fl oz) double cream
100 ml (3½ fl oz) milk
100 ml (3½ fl oz) golden syrup
400 g (14 oz) good quality dark
   chocolate, 70% cocoa solids

ROCKY ROAD TOPPING
2 handfuls soft caramel sweets
50 g (2 oz) pistachios
100 g (2 oz) salted peanuts
2 handfuls mini marshmallows

1. Make the brownies according to the basic recipe and let it cool before adding the topping.

Toppings
1. Boil the cream, milk and syrup. Remove the pan from the heat and let the liquid cool a few degrees.
2. Finely chop the chocolate and fold it into the warm cream, so the chocolate melts.
3. Spread the icing over the cake and sprinkle with chopped caramels, pistachios, peanuts and marshmallows.
4. Refrigerate until the icing is firm and then cut into squares.

devil's food peanut brownie

Devil's food cake is a classic American chocolate cake that is irresistible. This brownie is even better with its peanut butter frosting.

MAKES 24 SQUARES
1 portion brownie batter (see basic
   recipe page 96)

PEANUT BUTTER ICING
150 ml (5 fl oz) smooth peanut butter
500 g (18 oz) icing sugar
50 g (2 oz) good quality cocoa powder
1 tbsp vanilla sugar
300 g (10 oz) cream cheese
3 tbsp warm coffee
salted peanuts for garnish

1. Make the brownie batter according to the basic recipe and let it cool.

Icing
1. Whip the ingredients for the icing together with an electric mixer until smooth.
2. Spread the icing over the brownies and garnish with salted peanuts.

flourless brownie

This chocolatey flourless brownie is amazingly good and is the ultimate treat for gluten-intolerant guests. I like to serve it with a little lightly whipped cream.

MAKES 12 SQUARES

200 g (7 oz) butter

400 g (14 oz) good quality dark
   chocolate, 70% cocoa solids

6 free-range eggs

300 g (10 oz) sugar

1 vanilla pod, seeds scraped out

150 g (5 oz) walnuts, coarsely chopped,
   plus a few halves to decorate

75 g (3 oz) good quality cocoa powder

1 pinch sea salt

finely grated zest of 1 orange

lightly whipped cream, to serve

1. Preheat the oven to 180°C (350°F/gas 6).
2. Melt the butter and chocolate, mix until smooth and let cool.
3. Beat the eggs, sugar and vanilla seeds until white and fluffy.
4. Add the chopped walnuts, cocoa, salt and orange zest to the batter.
5. Carefully fold the melted chocolate and butter into it.
6. Place baking parchment on the bottom of a baking tin and fill the dish with the batter.
7. Garnish the surface with whole walnuts.
8. Bake the cake in the middle of the oven for 20–25 minutes. It should be firm when you carefully shake the tin, but soft in the middle, because otherwise it gets too crumbly.
9. Let the cake cool, slice it into squares and serve with cream.

brownie cupcakes

MAKES 12 CUPCAKES

200 g (7 oz) hazelnuts
175 g (6 oz) butter
150 g (5 oz) sugar
100 g (4 oz) muscovado sugar
75 g (3 oz) good quality cocoa powder
50 ml (2 fl oz) golden syrup
1 pinch salt
100 g (4 oz) plain flour
1 tsp baking powder
3 free-range eggs
100 g (4 oz) good quality dark
   chocolate, 70% cocoa slids
lightly whipped cream and fresh
   raspberries, to serve

1. Preheat the oven to 200°C (400°F/gas 6).
2. Roast the whole hazelnuts in the middle of the oven for 6–10 minutes. Let them cool, then rub away most of the skin with the help of a tea towel.
3. Beat the butter, sugar and muscovado sugar until creamy.
4. Mix in the cocoa, syrup and salt. Mix the flour with the baking powder.
5. Beat one egg at a time into the mixture and fold the flour in last.
6. Coarsely chop the chocolate and mix it together with the whole hazelnuts into the mixture.
7. Set out paper muffin cups in a muffin tin and fill the cups two-thirds full with batter.
8. Lower the oven temperature to 180°C (350°F/gas 4.
9. Bake in the middle of the oven for around 20 minutes. Test for doneness with a toothpick; they should be a little sticky in the middle.
10. Serve topped with whipped cream and fresh raspberries.

coconut swirl brownies

These are really moist brownies. The coconut makes it quite sweet and a little heavier.

MAKES 24 SQUARES

BROWNIE BATTER
500 g (18 oz) softened butter
200 g (7 oz) sugar
2 tbsp vanilla sugar
100 g (4 oz) good quality cocoa powder
100 ml (3½ oz) golden syrup
1 tsp salt
8 free-range eggs
175 g (6 oz) plain flour

COCONUT BATTER
4 tbsp sugar
200 ml (7 oz) double cream
250 g (9 oz) coconut flakes
4 egg whites
½ tbsp vanilla sugar
butter for greasing

1. Preheat the oven to 180°C (350°F/gas 4).
2. Beat together the butter, sugar and vanilla sugar until white and creamy.
3. Mix in the cocoa, syrup and salt.
4. Add the eggs, one at a time and then the flour last.
5. Make the coconut batter: mix the sugar, cream, coconut flakes, egg whites and vanilla sugar in a bowl.
6. Place baking parchment on the bottom of a baking tin and butter the sides.
7. Spread the brownie batter in the dish and spoon/drizzle the coconut batter over it.
8. Use a knife to draw a pattern through the cake, so it looks marbled.
9. Bake in the middle of the oven for around 25 minutes. Test for doneness in the middle of the cake; it should be a little sticky in the middle.
10. Let it cool and then cut into squares.

peanut butter swirl brownies

This is a real killer for chocoholics who love peanuts. The salt in the nuts is really good in combination with the sweet chocolate. You make the cake in two batters then layer them in a cake tin.

MAKES 24 SQUARES

BROWNIE BATTER

400 g (14 oz) softened butter

350 g (12 oz) sugar

2 tbsp vanilla sugar

100 g (4 oz) good quality cocoa powder

100 ml (3½ oz) golden syrup

3 pinches sea salt

8 free-range eggs

175 g (6 oz) plain flour

PEANUT BATTER

100 g (4 oz) butter

125 g (4½ oz) icing sugar

350 g (12 oz) peanut butter

2 pinches sea salt

1 tsp vanilla sugar

50 g (2 oz) salted peanuts

1. Preheat the oven to 180°C (350°F/gas 4).
2. Beat together the butter, sugar and vanilla sugar until white and creamy.
3. Mix in the cocoa, syrup and salt.
4. Add the eggs, one at a time and the flour last.
5. Make the peanut cream: melt the butter and whip it together with the icing sugar, peanut butter, salt and vanilla sugar. Let it cool but not harden.
6. Place baking parchment on the bottom of a baking tin and butter the sides.
7. Spread the brownie batter in the tin and spoon or drizzle the peanut batter over it.
8. Use a knife to draw a pattern through the cake, to create a marbled effect. Sprinkle with salted peanuts.
9. Bake in the middle of the oven for around 30 minutes. The cake should pull away from the walls and it should be firm.
10. Let it cool and then cut into squares.

blondies

A blondie is a light brownie. In America, they are made with brown sugar, which gives them their characteristic flavour. A blondie should be moist and a little chewy – I use white chocolate in my blondies and enjoy them with a glass of milk.

BASIC RECIPE
MAKES 24 SQUARES
450 g (1 lb) softened butter
200 g (7 oz) sugar
200 g (7 oz) light muscovado sugar
1 tbsp vanilla sugar
finely grated zest of 3 lemons
6 free-range eggs
500 g (18 oz) plain flour
1 tbsp baking powder
1 tsp salt
300 g (10 oz) good quality white chocolate

1. Preheat the oven to 180°C (350°F/gas 4).
2. Beat the butter, sugar, muscovado and vanilla sugar until white and creamy. Mix in the lemon zest then beat in one egg at a time.
3. Sift together the flour, baking powder and salt and fold it into the batter.
4. Coarsely chop the chocolate and mix it into the batter.
5. Place baking parchment on the bottom of a baking tin and fill the tin with the batter.
6. Bake in the middle of the oven for about 25 minutes.
7. Let the cake cool and then slice it into squares.

raspberry blondie

When I was in London once, I ate a fantastically good blondie with raspberries and coconut in it. This recipe is my variation. Of course you can put coconut in it too, if you want. Lime and coconut taste wonderful together.

MAKES 24 SQUARES
1 portion blondie batter (see basic recipe above)
finely grated zest of 4 limes (instead of lemon)
250 g (9 oz) fresh raspberries (instead of white chocolate)

1. Preheat the oven to 180°C (350°F/gas 4).
2. Make the blondie batter according to the basic recipe but replace the lemon zest with lime zest and leave out the white chocolate.
3. Place baking parchment on the bottom of a baking tin and fill the tin with the batter.
4. Make small indentations in the batter with your fingers and carefully press the raspberries into the holes.
5. Bake in the middle of the oven for about 25 minutes.
6. Let the cake cool and then slice it into squares.

moist coconut slice with lime

Sweet coconut meets sour lime in this blond, moist and exotic slice. It's like a little trip to the tropics and it will satisfy your cravings for sweets.

MAKES 24 SQUARES

450 g (1 lb) softened butter
500 g (18 oz) sugar
1 tbsp vanilla sugar
finely grated zest of 6 limes
6 free-range eggs
500 g (18 oz) flour
200 g (7 oz) coconut flakes
1 tbsp baking powder
1 tsp salt
3 tbsp Malibu liqueur (optional)

LIME ICINGING

125 g (4½ oz) softened butter
400 g (14 oz) icing sugar
2 tsp vanilla sugar
finely grated zest of 4 limes and juice
    of 1 lime
200 g (7 oz) cream cheese
lemon and lime zest to garnish

1. Preheat the oven to 180°C (350°F/gas 4).
2. Beat the butter, sugar and vanilla sugar together until creamy. Add the grated lime zest and the eggs one at a time.
3. Mix together the flour, coconut flakes, baking powder and salt and fold it into the batter.
4. Flavour with the liqueur if you are using it.
5. Place baking parchment on the bottom of a baking tin and fill the tin with the batter.
6. Bake in the middle of the oven for around 25 minutes.
7. Let the cake cool while you mix the frosting.

Icing

1. Beat together the butter, icing sugar, vanilla sugar, grated lime zest, lime juice and cream cheese until creamy.
2. Spread the frosting on the cake and cut it into oblong pieces.
3. Sprinkle with lemon and lime zest before serving.

pecan and cranberry bars

MAKES 26 SQUARES

450 g (1 lb) softened butter
250 g (9 oz) light muscovado sugar
2 tsp vanilla sugar
2 free-range eggs
600 g (1 lb 5 oz) plain flour
2 tsp baking powder
1 tsp bicarbonate of soda
2 tsp ground cinnamon
200 g (7 oz) pecan nuts, chopped
300 g (10 oz) dried cranberries

1. Preheat the oven to 180°C (350°F/gas 4).
2. Cream the butter, muscovado and vanilla sugar together until creamy, then mix in the eggs.
3. Mix together the flour, baking powder, bicarbonate of soda and cinnamon and fold it into the batter.
4. Fold the pecans and the cranberries into the batter.
5. Place baking parchment on the base of a baking tin (20 x 20 cm/8 x 8 in) and fill the tin with the batter.
6. Bake in the middle of the oven for around 30 minutes. Test for doneness with a toothpick or knife; it should be dry.
7. Let the cake cool and then cut it into oblong pieces

i scream
ice cream

The best thing about ice cream desserts is that I can make them in plenty of time before dinner. Then I can spend time with my guests instead of standing in the kitchen at the end of the meal. All I have to do is take the dessert out of the freezer and let it soften a little before serving. Making your own ice cream is unbelievably simple and you don't even need an ice cream maker. In this chapter, you'll find my best recipes for ice cream bombe, semifreddo and lots more.

five kinds of glace au four

Glace au four means 'ice cream in the oven' in French, while in America it is called Baked Alaska. This dessert made of sponge cake, ice cream and a meringue topping is assembled and then baked briefly in the oven, where the meringue keeps the ice cream from melting. What's nice about this 1970s cult dessert is that it's easy to vary. *Glace au four* is best with homemade sponge cake, fruit or berries and a little liqueur.

BASIC RECIPE
SERVES 8

SPONGE CAKE
3 free-range eggs
250 g (9 oz) sugar
1 tsp vanilla sugar
50 g (2 oz) butter
100 ml (3½ fl oz) milk
225 g (8 oz) plain flour
2 tsp baking powder
1 pinch salt
butter and bread crumbs for the dish

MERINGUE
3 free-range eggs
225 g (8 oz) sugar
4 drops fresh lemon juice

FILLING
fresh fruits and berries
liqueur or rum (optional)
1½ litres (2½ pints) vanilla ice cream

1. Preheat the oven to 180°C (350°F/gas 4).
2. For the sponge, whisk the eggs, sugar and vanilla sugar until white and really fluffy.
3. Melt the butter and add to the milk. Mix this with the eggs.
4. Mix the flour, baking powder and salt and carefully fold this into the mixture.
5. Pour the batter into a round cake tin that has been buttered and sprinkled with bread crumbs.
6. Bake the cake in the middle of the oven for around 30 minutes. Test for doneness with a toothpick or knife.
7. Let the cake cool, then turn out on a cooling rack.

1. For the meringue, separate the egg whites from the yolks.
2. Whisk the egg whites, sugar and lemon juice in a dry and clean stainless steel or glass bowl.
3. Whip the meringue hard by hand over a pan of boiling water until it reaches 65°C (150°F). The meringue should thicken and the sugar crystals melt.
4. Remove the meringue from the heat and continue to whip with an electric mixer until it has cooled.

1. To assemble: preheat the grill to 250°C (500°F/gas 10).
2. Slice the sponge into 2.5 cm (1 in) thick slices. Place in the bottom of a high-sided ovenproof dish.
3. Top the sponge layer with sliced fruits and berries. Drizzle with a little liqueur or rum, if you are using it.
4. Slice or scoop the ice cream over the fruit (the ice cream should be firm).
5. Spread the meringue so that it covers all the ice cream. Then put under the grill with the oven door open until the meringue has turned golden, about 4 minutes. Serve immediately, before the ice cream melts.

glace au four with rum-marinated berries and almond meringue

Rum and berries taste so good in this addictive dessert. It's almost impossible to stop eating it, that's how good it is.

SERVES 8

1 sponge cake (see basic recipe
    page 116)
1 portion meringue (see basic recipe
    page 116)
flaked almonds

FILLING

100 ml (3½ fl oz) water
200 g (7 oz) sugar
4 tbsp light rum
300 g (10 oz) fresh or frozen
    blackberries
300 g (10 oz) fresh or frozen
    raspberries
1½ litres (2½ pints) vanilla ice cream

1. Make the sponge cake according to the basic recipe.
2. Preheat the grill to 250°C (500°F/gas 10).
3. Make the meringue according to the basic recipe and fold in the flaked almonds.
4. Boil the water and sugar. Remove it from the heat and flavour with rum. Put the berries into the syrup and cool.
5. Slice the sponge into slices about 2.5 cm (1 in) thick. Place the slices in the bottom of a high-sided ovenproof dish.
6. Spoon the berries and some of the syrup over the sponge.
7. Slice the frozen ice cream into 2.5 cm (1 in) thick and place the slices in a layer over the berries (or you can scoop the ice cream over the berries).
8. Spread the meringue so it covers all the ice cream and grill it with the oven door open until the meringue has turned golden, about 4 minutes. Serve immediately.

banoffee glace au four

This is a really childish dessert, but oh so good. If you want a more adult taste, you can brush the sponge cake slices with a little syrup flavoured with a drop of rum.

SERVES 8

1 sponge cake (see basic recipe
    page 116)
1 portion meringue (see basic recipe
    page 116)

FILLING

2 ripe bananas, sliced
100 ml (3½ fl oz) caramel sauce
100 g (4 oz) walnuts, crushed
1½ litres (2½ pints) vanilla ice cream

1. Make the sponge cake according to the basic recipe.
2. Preheat the grill to 250°C (500°F/gas 10).
3. Make the meringue according to the basic recipe.
4. Slice the sponge into slices about 2.5 cm (1 in) thick. Place the slices in the bottom of a high-sided ovenproof dish.
5. Distribute the sliced bananas over the sponge cake. Drizzle with caramel sauce. Top with crushed walnuts.
6. Slice the frozen ice cream into 2.5 cm (1 in) thick and place the slices in a layer over the bananas (or you can scoop the ice cream over the bananas).
7. Spread the meringue so it covers all the ice cream and grill it with the oven door open until the meringue has turned golden, about 4 minutes. Serve immediately

glace au four with red summer berries and lime

You can even bake *glace au four* in individual dishes, ramekins or an ovenproof dish. Lime adds a delicious taste to sweet berries such as strawberries and raspberries.

SERVES 8

1 sponge cake (see basic recipe
    page 116)
1 portion meringue (see basic recipe
    page 116)

FILLING

450 g (1 lb) strawberries
250 g (9 oz) raspberries
50 g (2 oz) demerara sugar
finely grated zest of 2 limes and juice
    of 1 lime
1½ litres (2½ pints) vanilla ice cream

1. Make the sponge cake according to the basic recipe.
2. Preheat the grill to 250°C (500°F/gas 10).
3. Make the meringue according to the basic recipe.
4. Slice the sponge into slices about 2.5 cm (1 in) thick. Place the slices in the bottom of a high-sided ovenproof dish.
5. Mash the strawberries and mix them with the raspberries, sugar, zest from 2 limes and juice of 1 lime.
6. Distribute the berries over the sponge cake.
7. Slice the frozen ice cream into slices about 2.5 cm (1 in) thick and place the slices in a layer over the berries (or you can scoop the ice cream).
8. Spread the meringue so it covers all the ice cream and grill it with the oven door open until the meringue has turned golden, for about 4 minutes.

glace au four with the flavour of apple cake

This is like apple cake, but with a twist. It's best if you use really tart apples, because otherwise it gets too sweet.

SERVES 8

1 sponge cake (see basic recipe
    page 116)
1 portion meringue (see basic recipe
    page 116)

FILLING

5 large tart apples, peeled and sliced
    into wedges
½ tsp cardamom seeds
50 g (2 oz) butter
50 g (2 oz) sugar
1 tbsp ground cinnamon
100 g (4 oz) flaked almonds
1½ litres (2½ pints) vanilla ice cream

1. Make the sponge cake according to the basic recipe.
2. Pre-heat the grill to 250°C (500°F/gas 10).
3. Make the meringue according to the basic recipe.
4. Pound the cardamom in a mortar.
5. Fry the apples until soft in butter, sugar, cinnamon and cardamom. Roast the flakedd almonds in a dry frying pan.
6. Slice the sponge into slices about 2.5 cm (1 in) thick. Place the slices in the bottom of a high-sided ovenproof dish.
7. Distribute the fried apples over the sponge cake and sprinkle over the almonds.
8. Slice the frozen ice cream into slices about 2.5 cm (1 in) thick and place the slices in a layer over the apples (or you can scoop the ice cream over the apples).
9. Spread the meringue so it covers all the ice cream and grill it with the oven door open until the meringue has turned golden, for about 4 minutes.

ice cream bombe with raspberry meringue

This dessert can be partially prepared a few days before a party. About 20 minutes before serving, remove from the freezer to let the bombe (without the meringue) soften in the refrigerator. Turn the bombe out onto a serving tray. Then freeze the bombe again for 10 minutes so the surface can harden – do this so the meringue doesn't slide off. You have to work fast when you pipe the meringue since the ice cream melts quickly. You will need a blow torch to brown the meringue.

SERVES 8

2 litres (3½ pints) softened vanilla ice cream

¾ litre (1¼ pints) softened raspberry sorbet

1 cake base (ready-made is fine)

1 small metal bowl (¾ litre/1¼ pint capacity)

1 large metal bowl (2 litre/3½ pint capacity)

RASPBERRY MERINGUE

3 free-range egg whites

4 drops fresh lemon juice

325 g (11 oz) sugar

200 g (7 oz) fresh or frozen raspberries

1. For the bombe: freeze the bowls (so the ice cream sticks to the sides and does not melt as quickly when the bowls are being filled).
2. Soften the sorbet in the refrigerator for 20–30 minutes. Pack it firmly into the little metal bowl. Cover with clingfilm and freeze it until the sorbet is hard again, about 2 hours.
3. Soften the vanilla ice cream in the refrigerator for 20–30 minutes. Cover the bottom and walls of the larger metal bowl with vanilla ice cream so you leave the centre hollow.
4. Take the bowl with the raspberry sorbet out and dip the outside of the bowl quickly into hot water. Take the sorbet out and press it into the hollow space in the vanilla ice cream. Fill in any excess space with more vanilla ice cream and spread a layer of vanilla ice cream on top so the sorbet disappears into the middle of the bombe.
5. Cut a round slice out of the cake bottom so it covers the entire surface of the ice cream. Cover with clingfilm and freeze again until the ice cream bombe is hard.
6. Quickly dip the outside of the bowl into hot water and turn the ice cream out. Freeze it again so the surface freezes.

1. For the meringue: whisk the egg whites, lemon juice and 100 g (4 oz) of the sugar with an electric mixer into a thick meringue in a dry, clean stainless steel bowl.
2. Add another 100 g (4 oz) sugar while whipping it.
3. Mash the raspberries with the rest of the sugar and whip it into the meringue at low speed. Whip until it is firm.
4. Pipe or spread the meringue over the ice cream bombe and brown the surface with a blow torch.

not-too-difficult summer ice cream cake

This sweet, summery cake should be served slightly frozen. You shouldn't store it for more than a few days in the freezer because it easily absorbs the smell of the freezer. You can make it either with mascarpone or cream cheese. Both are wonderful.

SERVES 8
4 free-range eggs
200 g (7 oz) sugar
200 g (7 oz) mascarpone
400 ml (14 fl oz) double cream
1–2 meringue bases (bought is fine), broken into pieces
fresh white currants, to decorate

1. Separate the egg yolks from the whites.
2. Beat sugar and yolks until fluffy, then mix in the mascarpone.
3. Whip the cream until fluffy and fold it into the yolks.
4. Whip the egg whites until firm then fold into the mixture.
5. Layer meringue and the ice cream mixture in a jelly mold, starting with the ice cream and then layering in broken pieces of meringue.
6. Cover the cake with cling film and freeze for at least 5 hours.
7. Dip the outside of the mold into warm water to loosen the cake. Serve with whit or red currants or other berries.

train ice cream cake

Make one wagon at a time so the ice cream doesn't melt. Make the engine last since the cake shouldn't be in the freezer too long. I make my wagons on small rectangular trays and then put them together. It is a great way to avoid melted ice cream! Let the train stand in the refrigerator a little while before serving so the ice cream gets soft.

SERVES 12–14 CHILDREN
6 blocks vanilla ice cream (½ litre/1 pint blocks)
6 caramel sticks
1 bag small meringues
1 Swiss roll with jam
1 packet of round biscuits (for the wheels)
1 small jar of caramel sauce
mixed sweets for garnish (caramel sticks, M&Ms, raspberry jellies, etc)
icing sugar
cake candles

1. Begin by making two cars: place 2 ice cream blocks on each other and attach cookies as wheels. Repeat.
2. Place caramel sticks along the edge on top of the ice cream and fill with a load of crushed meringue. Repeat.
3. Drizzle a little caramel sauce over the meringue and sprinkle with sweets.
4. Engine: Make the engine out of 2 ice cream blocks on top of each other. Divide the Swiss roll in half, place one half on the ice cream for the boiler, then the other half upright to make the cab.
5. Dust the Swiss roll with icing sugar and make windshield wipers out of caramel sticks. Make a chimney out of sweets and headlights out of M&Ms...Let your imagination go wild!

dime bar ice cream cake with strawberries

This cake is a big favourite amongst kids and some adults too! Dime bar and ice cream are great together. And the addition of lime-sugared strawberries makes a really fresh and summery accompaniment that suits the cake perfectly.

SERVES 8
4 free-range eggs
50 g (2 oz) sugar
200 g (7 oz) cream cheese
300 ml (10 fl oz) double cream
3 double Dime bars, chopped to make about 150 g (5 oz) in total
200 g (7 oz) digestive biscuits, crushed

LIME STRAWBERRIES
1 kg (2 lb 2 oz) fresh strawberries
100 g (4 oz) demerara sugar
finely grated zest of 3 limes

1. Separate the egg yolks from the whites.
2. Whisk the egg yolks and sugar until fluffy and mix in the cream cheese.
3. Whip the cream until fluffy and fold it into the egg mixture.
4. Whip the egg whites into stiff peaks and carefully fold into the mixture.
5. Mix the chopped Dime bars into the mixture.
6. Crush the digestive biscuits and then layer the crumbs with the creamy mixture in a sponge cake mould.
7. Freeze the ice cream cake for about 5 hours, until it is lightly frozen.
8. Hull and slice the strawberries. Sprinkle the slices with the demerara sugar and grated lime zest and and serve them with the dime bar ice cream cake.

meringue suisse

SERVES 8
2 litres (3½ pints) vanilla ice cream
4 bananas, sliced
½ bag small meringues
500 ml (18 fl oz) whipping cream, lightly whipped
1 portion chocolate sauce (see recipe below)

CHOCOLATE SAUCE
25 g (1 oz) good quality cocoa powder
100 g (4 oz) sugar
50 ml (2 fl oz) water
1 tbsp oil

1. Layer the ice cream, sliced bananas and meringue in a bowl. Top with lightly whipped cream and drizzle with chocolate sauce (see method for sauce below).

1. For the sauce: mix the cocoa, sugar and water in a little pan and cook the chocolate sauce for about 3 minutes.
2. Add the oil and let cool.

nine kinds of semifreddo

Semifreddo means 'half-frozen' in Italian and it is a fantastic and easy-to-make ice cream dessert. It is quick to make and you don't need an ice cream maker – just whip the mixture together then freeze until half-frozen. I make it so it is a little soft in the middle – it is important not to freeze it overnight, otherwise it will be rock hard. If you want to make it ahead, let it thaw slowly in the refrigerator before serving.

BASIC RECIPE
SERVES 8
4 free-range eggs
100 g (4 oz) sugar
1 fresh vanilla pod, seeds scraped out
400 ml (14 fl oz) double cream

1. Separate the egg yolks from the whites.
2. Whisk the yolks with half the sugar and the seeds from the vanilla pod until white and fluffy.
3. Whip the cream until fluffy and fold it into the egg mixture.
4. Whip the egg whites with the rest of the sugar until stiff. Carefully folk this into the egg mixture.
5. Pour the ice cream into a freezer-safe dish, bowl or plastic box and freeze it for 3–4 hours so that it is half-frozen (soft in the middle).

strawberry semifreddo

SERVES 8
500 g (18 oz) fresh or frozen strawberries
50 ml (2 fl oz) water
200 g (7 oz) sugar
1 portion semifreddo (see basic recipe above)
300 ml (10 fl oz) thick Greek yogurt (to replace 200 ml/7 fl oz of the double cream)

1. Slice the strawberries if using fresh then simmer with water and sugar to make a loose compote, around 30 minutes.
2. Cool the compote well in the refrigerator.
3. Make the semifreddo according to the basic recipe, but replace 200 ml/7 fl oz of the cream with 300 ml/10 fl oz of Greek yogurt. Whip the cream until fluffy and fold it together with the yogurt.
4. Mix the compote into the semifreddo mixture.
5. Pour the mixture into a freezer-safe dish, bowl or plastic box and freeze it for 3–4 hours until it is half-frozen (soft in the middle).

tiramisu semifreddo

Tiramisu is an Italian dessert, the name of which means 'pick-me-up' because it contains caffeine in the form of cocoa and coffee. Here I've borrowed tiramisu's ingredients to enhance the flavour of a wonderful semifreddo. For the tiramisu, you need savoiardi biscuits (also known as sponge fingers). These oblong biscuits are available in well-stocked shops and supermarkets.

SERVES 8

1 portion semifreddo (see basic recipe
   page 128, but leave out the vanilla)
250 g (9 oz) mascarpone (to replace
   150 ml/5 fl oz cream)
100 ml (3½ fl oz) marsala wine
12 sponge finger
150 ml (5 fl oz) espresso
cocoa powder, to decorate

1. Make the semifreddo according to the basic recipe, but leave out the vanilla pod and reduce the amount of cream to 250 ml (9 fl oz).
2. Whisk the mascarpone with the marsala and carefully add the yolk, the whipped cream and the whipped egg whites.
3. Line an oblong loaf tin with clingfilm.
4. Put a little of the ice cream mixture into the bottom of the tin and dip one biscuit at a time into the cold espresso. Place a layer of biscuits in the tin and top with some of the ice cream. Repeat the procedure again.
5. Lightly tap the tin against the work surface so any air bubbles dissipate. Freeze it for 3–4 hours so that it is half frozen; it should still be a little soft in the middle.
6. Turn out the tiramisu onto a serving plate and remove the clingfilm. Dust with cocoa, to decorate.

chocolate semifreddo

Chocolate semifreddo can be flavoured in various ways. For example, you can use peppermint oil, liqueur or nuts. In this recipe, I've used Kahlúa, which is a coffee liqueur, but it is just as good with Amaretto, Frangelico, Bailey's, cognac, whisky or brandy, or any other flavoured alcohol you like.

SERVES 8

1 portion semifreddo (see basic recipe page 128)

200 ml (7 fl oz) thick Greek yogurt (instead of 200 ml/7 fl oz cream)

200 g (7 oz) good quality dark chocolate, 70% cocoa solids

2 tbsp Kahlúa (coffee liqueur)

1. Make the semifreddo according to the basic recipe, but replace 200 ml/7 fl oz of the cream with the Greek yogurt. Whisk the cream until fluffy then fold it into the Greek yogurt.
2. Break the chocolate into pieces and melt it in a bowl over a pan of boiling water (not touching the water).
3. Mix together the beaten egg yolks with the melted chocolate and liqueur. Fold in the cream and yogurt mixture and add the whipped egg whites last.
4. Pour the ice cream into a freezer-safe dish, bowl or plastic box and freeze it for 3–4 hours so that it is half-frozen or soft in the middle.

rhubarb semifreddo

To succeed with rhubarb semifreddo, first cook the rhubarb into a creamy compte with sugar and water. It is a lovely summery and refreshing ice cream to serve as a snack or as a dessert.

SERVES 8

about 5 long stalks of rhubarb

400 g (14 oz) sugar

50 ml (2 fl oz) water

1 portion semifreddo (see basic recipe page 128)

300 ml (10 fl oz) thick Greek yogurt (instead of 200 ml/7 fl oz of cream)

1. Cut the rhubarb into pieces about 3 cm (1½ in) long.
2. Cook the rhubarb with the sugar and water into a compote in a thick-bottomed pot, for about 30 minutes (the rhubarb should fall apart completely).
3. Cool the compote well and chill to refrigerator temperature.
4. Make the semifreddo according to the basic recipe, but replace 200 ml/7 fl oz of the cream with 300 ml/10 fl oz of Greek yogurt. Whip the cream until fluffy and fold it into the Greek yogurt.
5. Fold the compote into the ice cream mixture.
6. Pour the ice cream into a freezer-safe dish, bowl or plastic box and freeze it for 3–4 hours so that it is half-frozen or still soft in the middle.

berry semifreddo

SERVES 8

75 ml (3 fl oz) water
150 g (5 oz) sugar
400 g (14 oz) mixed berries
1 portion semifreddo (see basic recipe page 128)
2 handfuls meringues, lightly crushed
2 tbsp Grand Marnier (orange liqueur)

1. Boil the water and sugar in a pot, remove the pot from the heat and add the berries. Let them sit until the syrup has cooled completely.
2. Make the semifreddo according to the basic recipe. Fold in lightly crushed meringues and Grand Marnier.
3. Strain away the syrup and mix the berries into the mixture.
4. Pour the ice cream into an ovenproof, bowl or plastic box and freeze it for 3–4 hours so that it is half-frozen or still soft in the middle.

chunky monkey semifreddo

Chunky Monkey is a flavour of Ben & Jerry's ice cream, and it has inspired our tasty semifreddo of bananas, roasted walnuts and chocolate pieces. With the addition of a little meringue and rum, it can't be anything but a success. Rum is a good flavouring but obviously ought to be left out if this semifreddo is served to children.

SERVES 8

100 g walnuts, chopped

1 portion semifreddo (see basic recipe page 128)

3 ripe bananas

150 g (5 oz) good quality dark chocolate, 70% cocoa solids

2 handfuls meringue, coarsely crushed

2 tbsp light rum (optional)

1. Roast the nuts in a dry frying pan and cool completely.
2. Make the semifreddo according to the basic recipe. Dice 2 bananas into small pieces and mash the third. Mix them with the whipped cream.
3. Coarsely chop the chocolate and nuts.
4. Fold the crushed meringues, nuts and chocolate into the ice cream mixture. Flavour with rum if desired.
5. Pour into a freezer-safe dish, bowl or plastic box and freeze for 3–4 hours until half frozen or soft in the middle.

apple and yogurt semifreddo

SERVES 8

1 portion semifreddo (see basic recipe page 128)

50 g (2 oz) sugar

finely grated zest of 1 lemon

200 ml (7 fl oz) thick Greek yogurt (instead of 200 ml/7 fl oz cream)

150 ml (5 fl oz) apple sauce

1. Make the semifreddo according to the basic recipe and add the extra sugar plus grated lemon zest when the yolks are being beaten.
2. Replace 200 ml (7 fl oz) cream with the Greek yogurt. Whip the cream until fluffy and fold it into the Greek yogurt and the apple sauce.
3. Pour into a freezer-safe dish, bowl or plastic box and freeze for 3–4 hours until half frozen or soft in the middle.

mango semifreddo

Since having a child, I have discovered the joys of fruit purées in jars! There are really good mango and other fruit purées that make great bases for drinks and desserts.

SERVES 8

1 portion semifreddo (see basic recipe page 128)

200 ml (7 fl oz) mango purée

finely grated zest of 1 lime (instead of vanilla pod)

200 ml (7 fl oz) thick Greek yogurt (instead of 200 ml/7 fl oz cream)

1. Make the semifreddo according to the basic recipe, but replace the vanilla with mango purée and grated lime zest, and replace 200 ml (7 fl oz) cream with the Greek yogurt.
2. Whip 200 ml (7 fl oz) cream until fluffy. Fold it into the Greek yogurt.
3. Mix the mango purée and the lime zest into the mixture.
4. Pour into a freezer-safe dish, bowl or plastic box and freeze for 3–4 hours until half-frozen or soft in the middle.

i scream ice cream

boulangerie

Baking your own bread is simple and there are lots of us who bake using sourdough
starter. You can make a sourdough stater yourself or you can cheat by buying some from
a bakery. Then you just keep it alive by feeding it now and then with fresh water and flour.
In my sourdough breads, I also use a little fresh yeast to get the fermentation process
going. Here are my tastiest breads, made both with and without sourdough starter.

nine kinds of baguette

The baguette is probably the world's most beloved and well-known bread. In France, bread is baked with much care – there's even an organization to ensure the bread is baked to a particular standard. There, the notches in the bread mean something and each bakery has its own way of notching the baguette.

BASIC RECIPE
MAKES 4 BAGUETTES
DOUGH ONE (STARTER)
5 g (¼ oz) fresh yeast
300 ml (10 fl oz) cold water
325 g (11 oz) strong bread flour

DOUGH TWO
15 g (½ oz) fresh yeast
300 ml (10 fl oz) cold water
1 portion dough one (starter)
1 tbsp salt
1 tbsp sugar
450–550 g (1 lb–1 lb 4 oz) strong bread
    flour
oil for the trays
sea salt

1. For the starter: crumble the yeast in a mixing bowl and dissolve it in the water.
2. Add the flour and mix it until the loose dough is smooth.
3. Cover the bowl with clingfilm and let it rise for at least 4 hours at room temperature or overnight in the refrigerator.

1. For dough two: crumble the yeast in a mixing bowl, add the water and mix.
2. Add dough one, salt, sugar and then the flour until the dough holds together. Work the dough in a mixer at low speed for around 15 minutes.
3. Let the dough rise under a cloth for around 1½ hours.
4. Preheat the oven to 240°C (475°F/gas 9).
5. Turn the dough out onto a well-floured surface, divide it into four pieces and carefully press each piece into a rectangle with your fingers.
6. Fold in a long side of each rectangle, roll it up and shape the ends into points.
7. Twist the baguettes once and place them on a well-oiled baguette tray (or a regular baking tray).
8. Let them rise under a cloth for about an hour.
9. Brush the baguettes with water and sprinkle with sea salt. Make a few incisions diagonally across each baguette with a sharp knife and immediately put the tray in the middle of the hot oven.
10. When the baguettes have coloured a little, lower the temperature to 200°C (400°F/gas 6).
11. Bake until the breads have been in the oven for a total of around 30 minutes, then let them cool on a rack.

rye baguette

Baguettes don't always have to be light. If you use a heavier type of grain, you get a wonderful character to your bread. But use some wheat flour, otherwise you won't get enough air bubbles in the bread.

BASIC RECIPE
MAKES 4 BAGUETTES
DOUGH ONE (STARTER)
5 g (¼ oz) fresh yeast
300 ml (10 fl oz) cold water
325 g (11 oz) strong bread flour

DOUGH TWO
15 g (½ oz) fresh yeast
300 ml (10 fl oz) cold water
1 portion dough one (starter)
1 tbsp salt
1 tbsp sugar
60 g (2¼ oz) rye sourdough starter
   (see recipe page 149)
25 g (1 oz) sunflower seeds
25 g (1 oz) cracked rye
60 g (2¼ oz) graham flour
350–400 g (12–14 oz) strong bread flour
coarse rye flour, to sprinkle on the
   work surface
oil for the trays

1. For the starter: crumble the yeast in a mixing bowl and dissolve it in the water.
2. Add the flour and mix it until the loose dough is smooth.
3. Cover the bowl with clingfilm and let it rise for at least 4 hours at room temperature or overnight in the refrigerator.

1. For dough two: crumble the yeast in a mixing bowl, add the water and mix.
2. Add dough one, salt, sugar, rye sourdough, sunflower seeds, cracked rye, graham flour and then the strong flour last until the dough holds together. Work the dough in a mixer at low speed for around 15 minutes.
3. Let the dough rise under a cloth for around 1½ hours.
4. Preheat the oven to 240°C (475°F/gas 9).
5. Turn the dough over onto a well-floured surface, ideally using coarse rye flour, then divide into four pieces and carefully press each piece into a rectangle with your fingers.
6. Fold in a long side of each rectangle, roll it up and shape the ends into points.
7. Twist the baguettes once and place them on a well-oiled baguette tray (or a regular baking tray).
8. Let them rise under a cloth for about an hour.
9. Brush the baguettes with water and sprinkle with sea salt. Make a few incisions diagonally across each baguette with a sharp knife and immediately put the tray in the middle of the hot oven.
10. When the baguettes have gained a little colour, lower the temperature to 200°C (400°F/gas 6).
11. Bake until the breads have been in the oven for a total of around 30 minutes, then cool on a rack.

beetroot baguette with feta

MAKES 4 BAGUETTES

1 portion baguette dough (see basic
    recipe for baguette of your choice)
75–150 g (3–5 oz) strong bread flour (in
    addition to that in basic recipe)
2 beetroot, peeled and coarsely grated
300 g (3 oz) feta cheese, crumbled
oil for greasing
sea salt

1. Preheat the oven to 240°C (475°F/gas 9).
2. Make the baguette dough according to the basic recipe. Add
   the grated beetroot to the dough and knead in two-thirds of
   the feta (save the rest to sprinkle over the baguettes before
   baking them).
3. Shape the dough and let the baguettes rise on a tray
   according to the basic recipe.
4. Brush with water, sprinkle with sea salt and remaining feta
   and immediately place the tray in the middle of the oven.
5. When the baguettes have gained a little colour, lower the
   temperature to 200°C (400°F/gas 6).
6. Bake until the breads have been in the oven for a total of
   around 30 minutes, then let them cool on a rack.

birdie num-num baguette

MAKES 4 BAGUETTES

1 portion baguette dough (see basic
    recipe for baguette of your choice)
50 g (2 oz) mixed seeds – poppy,
    sesame, sunflower and pumpkin
oil for greasing
sea salt

1. Preheat the oven to 240°C (475°F/gas 9).
2. Make the baguettes according to the basic recipe and let
   them rise on a greased tray.
3. Brush with water, sprinkle with seeds and sea salt.
4. Immediately place the tray in the middle of the oven.
5. When the baguettes have gained a little colour, lower the
   temperature to 200°C (400°F/gas 6).
6. Bake until the breads have been in the oven for a total of
   around 30 minutes, then let them cool on a rack.

rosemary baguette

MAKES 4 BAGUETTES

1 portion baguette dough (see basic
    recipe for baguette of your choice)
6 sprigs rosemary, leaves stripped and
    finely chopped
oil for greasing
sea salt

1. Preheat the oven to 240°C (475°F/gas 9).
2. Make the baguettes according to the basic recipe. Knead
   two-thirds of the finely chopped rosemary into the dough.
3. Shape the dough and let the baguettes rise on a tray
   according to the basic recipe.
4. Brush with water, sprinkle with sea salt and the rest of the
   chopped rosemary. Make some diagonal incisions in each
   baguette and place the tray in the middle of the oven.
5. When the baguettes have gained a little colour, lower the
   temperature to 200°C (400°F/gas 6).
6. Bake until the breads have been in the oven for a total of
   around 30 minutes, then let them cool on a rack.

onion baguette

These baguettes have a perfect, mild oniony taste. They are great for picnics when stuffed with delicious fillings or for serving with soup.

MAKES 4 BAGUETTES

1 portion baguette dough (see basic recipe page 138)

2 large onions, finely chopped and fried in butter

125 g (4½ oz) strong bread flour (in addition to that in the basic recipe)

2 tbsp butter

oil for greasing

1 large onion, sliced into rings

sea salt

1. Preheat the oven to 240°C (475°F/gas 9).
2. Make the baguettes according to the basic recipe. Knead fried and finely chopped onion into the dough along with the extra flour.
3. Shape the dough and let the baguettes rise on a tray according to the basic recipe.
4. Slice the other onion into rings.
5. Brush the baguettes with water and sprinkle with onion rings and sea salt.
6. Immediately place the tray in the middle of the oven.
7. When the baguettes have gained a little colour, lower the temperature to 200°C (400°F/gas 6).
8. Bake until the breads have been in the oven for a total of around 30 minutes, then let them cool on a rack.

olive baguette

MAKES 4 BAGUETTES

1 portion baguette dough (see basic recipe for baguette of your choice)

200 g (7 oz) black olives, stoned

oil for greasing

sea salt

1. Preheat the oven to 240°C (475°F/gas 9).
2. Make the baguette dough according to the basic recipe. Stone the olives and chop two-thirds of them. Knead the chopped olives into the dough by hand.
3. Thinly slice the rest of the olives and save these to sprinkle over the baguettes.
4. Shape the dough and let the baguettes rise on a tray according to the basic recipe.
5. Brush with water and sprinkle with sea salt and remaining sliced olives and immediately place the tray in the middle of the oven.
6. When the baguettes have gained a little colour, lower the temperature to 200°C (400°F/gas 6).
7. Bake until the breads have been in the oven for a total of around 30 minutes, then let them cool on a rack.

chocolate baguette

I first ate a chocolate baguette in Paris. It's an almost religious experience for a chocolate-lover. They are perfect for afternoon tea, breakfast or whenever.

MAKES 4 BAGUETTES

1 portion baguette dough (see basic recipe page 138)

100 ml (3½ fl oz) milk (in place of 100 ml/3½ fl oz of water from the basic recipe)

1 free-range egg

300 g (10 oz) good quality dark chocolate, 70% cocoa solids

oil for the trays

sea salt

1. Make the baguette dough according to the basic recipe but replace water with milk and add 1 egg to the dough. Carefully add coarsely chopped chocolate after all the flour has been added. Do not knead it (or the bread will turn brown).
2. Shape the dough and let the baguettes rise on a tray according to the basic recipe.
3. Preheat the oven to 240°C (475°F/gas 9).
4. Brush the baguettes with water and sprinkle with sea salt.
5. Make some incisions diagonally in each baguette with a sharp knife and place the tray in the middle of the oven.
6. When the baguettes have gained a little colour, lower the temperature to 200°C (400°F/gas 6).
7. Bake until the breads have been in the oven for a total of around 30 minutes, then let them cool on a rack.

baguette with fruit and nuts

This bread with dried fruit and nuts is perfect on a cheese board. It is also a juicy and tasty picnic bread and wonderful when used to make cheese sandwiches. Don't forget the chutney.

MAKES 4 BAGUETTES

1 portion baguette dough (see basic recipe page 138 for baguette of your choice)

200 g (7 oz) dried fruit (apricots, figs, raisins), coarsely chopped

50 g (2 oz) hazelnuts, chopped

50 g (2 oz) walnuts, chopped

oil for greasing

sea salt

1. Preheat the oven to 240°C (475°F/gas 9).
2. Make the baguette dough according to the basic recipe. Place the dried fruit in water at the same time as you make dough one (starter). Strain away the water and coarsely chop the fruits and nuts. Knead them in by hand.
3. Shape the dough and let the baguettes rise on a tray according to the basic recipe.
4. Brush the baguettes with water, sprinkle with sea salt and immediately place the tray in the middle of the oven.
5. When the baguettes have gained a little colour, lower the temperature to 200°C (400°F/gas 6).
6. Bake until the breads have been in the oven for a total of around 30 minutes, then let them cool on a rack.

wheat sourdough starter

BASIC RECIPE

ABOUT 1 LITRE (35 FL OZ)

DAY 1

200 ml (7 fl oz) lukewarm water

175 g (6 oz) flour

1 tbsp honey, clear

DAY 3

100 ml (3½ fl oz) lukewarm water

100 g (4 oz) flour

DAY 4

100 ml (3½ fl oz) lukewarm water

100 g (4 oz) flour

1. On Day 1 whisk the water, flour and honey for day 1 into a smooth mixture in a glass jar. Cover with clingfilm and let it stand at room temperature for 2 days.
2. On Day 3 add the water and flour for day 3 and whisk the mixture until smooth again. Cover with clingfilm and let it stand at room temperature for 1 day.
3. On Day 4 add the water and flour for day 4 and whisk the mixture until smooth. Cover with clingfilm and let it stand at room temperature for 1 day.

rye sourdough starter

BASIC RECIPE

ABOUT 1 LITRE (35 FL OZ)

DAY 1

200 ml (7 fl oz) lukewarm water

175 g (6 oz) rye flour

1 tbsp honey, clear

DAY 3

100 ml (3½ fl oz) lukewarm water

75 g (3 oz) rye flour

DAY 4

100 ml (3½ fl oz) lukewarm water

75 g (3 oz) rye flour

1. On Day 1 whisk the water, flour and honey for day 1 into a smooth mixture in a glass jar. Cover with clingfilm and let it stand at room temperature for 2 days.
2. On Day 3 add the water and flour for day 3 and whisk the mixture until smooth again. Cover with clingfilm and let it stand at room temperature for 1 day.
3. On Day 4 add the water and flour for day 4 and whisk the mixture until smooth again. Cover with clingfilm and let it stand at room temperature for 1 day.

good things to know about sourdough

Sourdough is comprised of flour and water that you mix and let stand for a few days until the natural yeasts and lactic acid bacteria grow. People use wheat flour or rye flour most often, but you can also use other types of flours, or a combination of flours. Once this happens it is known as the sourdough starter. The starter has to be stored in the refrigerator when it isn't being used, because it goes bad if it is kept at room temperature for too long. The dough (the bacteria) rests in the fridge.

You have to keep the sourdough starter alive and feed it occasionally with a little flour and water. It will then survive for a long time. A sourdough starter should have a pH value of under 4.0. But if it just stands in the fridge, eventually the production of lactic acid bacteria stops. By adding a little flour and water, the lactic acid bacteria gets going again. The more activity in the sourdough the better, because if there is more bacteria, the dough rises better.

The night before the sourdough is going to be used in bread-making, feed it and leave it out at room temperature overnight. The warmth makes the bacteria multiply, so the sourdough starts bubbling. That's a clear sign of life.

How to keep and use sourdough

It is hard to say exactly how much flour and water is needed to feed the starter because different types of flour absorb different amounts of liquid. Usually, you can feed the sourdough the same amount of water and flour, but some people prefer their sourdough loose and others thick.

Sourdough is mould-resistant but does not like be close to yeast. Yeast makes sourdough unbalanced, and then the yeast's bacteria take over. This makes the baked product worse and causes the dough to be harder to work with. So ideally keep fresh yeast in an air-tight plastic container if stored in the same refrigerator as sourdough starter.

Why sourdough?

Sourdough improves fermentation and increases the quality of the bread. It gives the bread a good, fresh, tart taste and a pleasant chewiness. The bread has tight pores and an elastic and juicy crumb.

Sourdough bread with rye flour is considered to be healthier because the sourdough processes break down the acids in the flour so the various nutrients are more easily accessible for the body. Also, sourdough bread lasts longer than ordinary bread.

Smart tips for the beginner

With sourdough, unprocessed organic or stone-ground flour is preferable because they have more micronutrients, minerals and natural wild yeast spores, which makes it easier for the fermentation process to get going.

To hurry the process, you can use yogurt, raw, grated apple or potato, honey, mashed grapes or raisins in the sourdough. During the cold parts of the year, it can be a good idea to warm the sourdough to give it a good start. Find a warm place in the kitchen (such as an oven that isn't on or on top of the refrigerator) for it to warm up.

Sourdough grows rapidly at room temperature so make sure you have big enough jars or containers. If it is stored in a jar, the lid shouldn't be screwed on completely. Sourdough needs oxygen in order to be active and grow.

If you don't succeed with your own sourdough or if you don't have time, you can buy sourdough from a bakery. Since these are fed regularly, they usually rise well, producing good bread.

levain bread

Levain is the French word for sourdough. It is simply a light bread baked from sourdough starter made from wheat or rye. I also use just a pinch of fresh yeast in my sourdough, just to get fermentation going. Despite its apparent simplicity, *levain* is not always easy to make, because you have to get the characteristic large bubbles into the bread. Therefore, the bread should rise a long time and be handled carefully so the air isn't pressed out.

MAKES 1 LARGE LOAF
10 g (1/3 oz) fresh yeast
600 ml (1 pt) lukewarm water
900–975 g (2 lb–2 lb 3 oz) strong bread flour
400 ml (14 fl oz) wheat sourdough starter
1/2 tbsp salt

1. Crumble the yeast in a mixing bowl and dissolve it in water. Add half the flour and knead it in a mixer for around 10 minutes.
2. Add the sourdough starter, salt and the rest of the flour. Knead at low speed for around 20 minutes.
3. Let the dough rise in a mixing bowl under a cloth until it doubles in size, about 2 hours.
4. Preheat the oven to 250°C (500°F/gas 10).
5. Place the dough on a floured wooden surface and shape it carefully into a loaf. Avoid working the dough, and handle it carefully so the air bubbles aren't pressed out. Flour the bread and let it rise under a cloth until it doubles in size, about 1 1/2 hours.
6. Put the bread on a tray and place it in the oven. Throw 75 ml (3 oz) of water on the bottom of the oven (to get a fine crackled crust). Lower the heat to 200°C (400°F/gas 6) and bake for 40–50 minutes.

corn bread

MAKES 3 LOAVES
700 g (1 lb 9 oz) corn (tinned is fine)
20 g (¾ oz) fresh yeast
700 ml (25 fl oz) lukewarm water
3 tbsp salt
100 ml (3½ fl oz) olive oil
2 tsp golden syrup
300 ml (10 fl oz) wheat sourdough
125 g (4½ oz) durum wheat flour
150 g (5 oz) polenta
1.1 kg (2 lb 7 oz) strong bread flour
butter and polenta

1. Drain the corn well and process half of it in a mixer.
2. Crumble the yeast in a mixing bowl and dissolve it in water. Add the salt, oil, syrup, sourdough starter and all the corn.
3. Add the durum wheat flour, polenta and the strong flour a little at a time.
4. Knead the dough at medium speed in the mixer for about 15 minutes until it is soft and elastic.
5. Sprinkle with flour and let the dough rise in the mixing bowl under a cloth until it doubles in size, about 1–2 hours.
6. Preheat the oven to 250°C (500°F/gas 10).
7. Shape the dough into 3 fat loaves and roll these in polenta.
8. Butter three loaf tins with softened butter and sprinkle with polenta. Place the loaves in them and let rise until double the size, about 1 hour.
9. Cut a long oblong notch in the middle of each loaf.
10. Put the bread in the middle of the oven and throw 75 ml (3 fl oz) of water on the bottom of the oven (to get a fine, crackled crust). Lower the heat to 200°C (400°F/gas 6) and bake for about 45 minutes. Turn the breads out of the tins and let cool on a rack.

cheese bread

MAKES 18 ROLLS

25 g (1 oz) fresh yeast
500 ml (18 fl oz) lukewarm water
1³/₄ tbsp sea salt
2 tsp honey
2 tsp golden syrup
100 ml (3¹/₂ oz) olive oil
100 ml (3¹/₂ oz) wheat sourdough
   starter
125 g (4¹/₂ oz) durum wheat flour
750 g (1 lb 10 oz) strong bread flour
200 g (7 oz) mature hard cheese
   (Cheddar type), grated
200 g (7 oz) feta cheese, crumbled
oil for greasing
sea salt, dried oregano and grated
   hard cheese to sprinkle on top

1. Crumble the yeast in a mixing bowl and dissolve it in water. Add sea salt, honey, syrup, olive oil and sourdough starter.
2. Add the durum flour and strong flour a little at a time and knead (at medium speed in a mixer) for around 10 minutes until the dough is smooth and elastic.
3. Sprinkle with a little flour and let the dough rise in the mixing bowl under a cloth until it doubles in size, 1¹/₂–2 hours.
4. Divide the dough in two, press or roll each piece into a rectangle and sprinkle both with plenty of grated cheese and crumbled feta. Roll each up, from one long side to the other.
5. Brush a tray with oil. Slice each roll into 9 slices and place them on the tray with the cut side upwards, with about 1 cm (¹/₂ in) between them (the rolls will rise into each other).
6. Preheat the oven to 200°C (400°F/gas 6).
7. Let the rolls rise under a cloth for around 45 minutes.
8. Brush the rolls with a little water, sprinkle with sea salt, oregano and grated cheese.
9. Bake in the middle of the oven for 20–25 minutes.

manhattan sourdough

MAKES 2 LOAVES

20 g (³/₄ oz) fresh yeast
700 ml (25 fl oz) lukewarm water
2¹/₂ tbsp salt
300 ml (10 fl oz) wheat sourdough
   starter
975 g (2 lb 3 oz) strong bread flour

1. Crumble the yeast in a mixing bowl and dissolve it in water. Add salt and sourdough starter.
2. Add a little flour at a time and knead the dough at medium speed in a mixer for about 15 minutes, until soft and elastic.
3. Sprinkle with a little flour and let the dough rise in the mixing bowl under a cloth until it doubles in size, about 2¹/₂ hours.
4. Preheat the oven to 250°C (500°F/gas 10).
5. Divide the dough in 2. Carefully shape them into plump loaves, flour them well and place in loaf tins. Let them rise until double in size, about 1¹/₂ hours.
6. Put the bread in the middle of the oven and throw 100 ml (3¹/₂ oz) water on the bottom of the oven (to get a fine, crackled crust). Lower the heat to 200°C (400°F/gas 6) and bake for about 50 minutes.

rustic greek bread

MAKES 2 LOAVES

25 g (1 oz) fresh yeast

800 ml (28 fl oz) lukewarm water

2½ tbsp salt

600 ml (1 pint) wheat sourdough
   starter

2 tbsp golden syrup

1.3 kg (3 lb) strong bread flour

1. Crumble the yeast in a mixing bowl and dissolve it in water.
   Add salt, sourdough starter and syrup.
2. Adding a little flour at a time, knead the dough at medium
   speed in a mixer for about 15 minutes, until soft and elastic.
3. Let the dough rise in the mixing bowl under a cloth until it
   doubles in size, about 2 hours.
4. Preheat the oven to 250°C (500°F/gas 10).
5. Knead the dough and shape it into two round loaves and
   place them on a tray lined with baking parchment. Sprinkle
   with flour and let rise until double in size, about 1½ hours.
6. Make three diagonal incisions in each loaf with a knife and
   place the tray in the middle of the oven. Throw 100 ml
   (3½ fl oz) water on the bottom of the oven to get a fine
   crackled crust. Lower the heat to 220°C (425°F/gas 7) and
   bake for 40–50 minutes until the bread is well coloured.

rye sourdough with apple and walnuts

This wonderful sourdough bread has a delicious crust and a slightly chewy crumb. Its yummy, sweet and fresh apple taste goes well with the walnuts and I like to serve it as a breakfast bread or with a cheese board. It is absolutely one of my favourites.

MAKES 2 LOAVES

25 g (1 oz) fresh yeast
600 ml (1 pint) lukewarm water
2½ tbsp salt
4 tbsp honey
75 ml rye sourdough starter
400 g (14 oz) rye flour
125 g (4½ oz) coarse rye flour
300–400 g (10–14 oz) strong bread flour
200 g (4 oz) walnuts, coarsely chopped
2 large apples, peeled, cored and
    finely diced

1. Crumble the yeast in a mixing bowl and dissolve it in water. Add salt, honey and sourdough starter.
2. Add the flours a little at a time.
3. Knead the dough at medium speed in the mixer for about 10 minutes, until it is elastic.
4. Carefully add the walnuts and apples to the dough by hand.
5. Sprinkle with a little flour and cover the dough in the mixing bowl with a cloth. Let it rise until double in size, about 1½ hours.
6. Knead the dough and shape it into two round breads. Let these rest for 10 minutes.
7. Preheat the oven to 250°C (500°F/gas 10).
8. Set the dough out lightly and shape into a loaf. Roll the ends so they are pointy and place the bread seam down on a well-floured cutting board.
9. Let the breads rise under a cloth until they double in size, for about 1–1½ hours.
10. Turn the breads over and lift them onto a tray. Make an incision in each with a knife.
11. Put the bread in the middle of the oven and throw 100 ml (3½ fl oz) water on the bottom of the oven to get a fine, crackled crust. Lower the heat to 220°C (425°F/gas 7) and bake for about 35 minutes.

croissants

Croissant means 'crescent' in French and these pastries are made of pastry layered with butter, which makes it flaky and crispy. If you like chocolate, it's yummy to fill the croissant with Nutella. Croissants are made in stages over two days.

MAKES 18 CROISSANTS

500 g (18 oz) strong bread flour

75 g (3 oz) sugar

1 tbsp salt

20 g (3/4 oz) fresh yeast

200 ml (7 fl oz) semi-skimmed milk

100 ml (3 1/2 fl oz) water

500 g (18 oz) butter, refrigerator
temperature

1 egg, beaten, for brushing

DAY 1

1. Sift the flour onto the work surface, make a well in the flour and put the sugar and salt into the well.
2. Crumble the yeast into a bowl and dissolve it in milk and water, then add the liquid to the well. Pinch the ingredients together and work the mixture until it is a smooth dough, about 5 minutes. Shape the dough into a ball, put in a bowl or plastic container with a lid.
3. Cover with clingfilm or a lid and let it rest in the refrigerator for at least 12 hours or overnight.

DAY 2

1. Roll out the butter between two sheets of greaseproof paper into a thick slab.
2. Slice a cross into the dough ball, fold out the edges and roll the dough out until it is 1/2 cm (1/2 inch) thick.
3. Place the slab of butter in the middle of the dough and roll the edges over the butter so it is covered.
4. Roll the dough out on a well-floured surface to 70 x 40 cm (16 x 28 inches). Brush off the excess flour. Fold the dough in 3 into a parcel.
5. Repeat rolling out and folding. Cover the dough with clingfilm and rest for 30 minutes in the refrigerator.
6. Repeat rolling out and folding. Cover the dough with clingfilm and let it rest for another 30 minutes in the refrigerator.
7. Roll the dough out very thin. It should be a sheet of about 70 x 40 cm (16 x 28 inches). Cut out 19 triangles.
8. Roll each triangle into croissants, starting with the wide end. Place the point underneath the croissant. Preheat the oven to 180°C (350°F/gas 4).
9. Bend croissants lightly and place on a tray lined with baking parchment. Cover with a cloth and let rise until double in size, about 1 1/2 hours.
10. Brush with beaten egg.
11. Bake until golden for 15–18 minutes.

olive bread

This tasty olive bread is a delicious accompaniment to food. It is great with soup, as a grilled sandwich and as a picnic bread. The dough is rather loose, so use a lot of flour on the table and work the dough until it feels a little firmer. This prevents the dough from moving around too much and helps the bread keep its shape in the oven.

MAKES 2 LOAVES

20 g (3/4 oz) fresh yeast

700 ml (25 fl oz) lukewarm water

2 tbsp salt

100 ml (3 1/2 oz) olive oil

2 tsp golden syrup

300 ml (10 fl oz) wheat sourdough starter

200 g (7 oz) durum wheat flour

750–900 g (1 lb 10 oz–2 lb) strong bread flour

200 g (7 oz) black olives, stoned and coarsely chopped

1. Crumble the yeast in a mixing bowl and dissolve it in water. Add salt, olive oil, syrup and sourdough starter.
2. Add the durum flour and strong flour a little at a time and knead the dough at medium speed in a mixer for about 10 minutes, until it is soft and elastic.
3. Knead the chopped olives into the dough by hand.
4. Sprinkle with a little flour and cover the dough in the mixing bowl with a cloth. Let it rise until it doubles in size, for about 2 hours.
5. Preheat the oven to 250°C (500°F/gas 10).
6. Knead the dough lightly on a well-floured surface. Divide in two and shape into round loaves. Place the loaves on a tray lined with baking parchment, sprinkle with a little flour and let rise under a cloth until double in size, about 1–1 1/2 hours.
7. Make an incision in the loaves and place the tray in the middle of the oven. Throw 100 ml (3 1/2 fl oz) water on the bottom of the oven to get a fine, crackled crust. Lower the heat to 220°C (425°F/gas 7) and bake for about 45 minutes.

spelt bread

Since spelt is a harder type of flour, I usually mix it with strong bread flour otherwise the resulting loaf is too hard. I make this bread in a round shape and let it rise on a floured wooden plank. While it's rising, I turn the loaves clockwise a few centimetres (inches) at a time, in order to get a beautiful pattern on them.

MAKES 2 LOAVES
20 g (3/4 oz) fresh yeast
700 ml (25 fl oz) lukewarm water
2 tbsp salt
300 ml (10 fl oz) wheat sourdough
   starter
275 g (13 oz) spelt flour
450–700 g (1 lb–1 lb 9 oz) strong
   bread flour
125 g (4 1/2 oz) spelt flakes

1. Crumble the yeast in a mixing bowl and dissolve it in water. Add salt and sourdough starter.
2. Work in the spelt flour and strong flour a little at a time. Add the spelt flakes.
3. Knead the dough at medium speed in a mixer for about 12 minutes, until it is elastic.
4. Sprinkle with a little flour and cover the dough in the mixing bowl with a cloth. Let it rise until double in size, for 2–3 hours.
5. Preheat the oven to 250°C (500°F/gas 10).
6. Knead the dough and shape it into 2 loaves. Place them on a well-floured wooden cutting board. Let rise under a cloth for 1–1 1/2 hours. 'Fluff' the breads while they're rising by turning the loaves regularly in the same direction. Turning them makes a beautiful pattern when you turn the loaves over onto the tray before baking them.
7. Put the breads on a tray lined with baking parchment and place them in the middle of the oven. Throw 100 ml (3 1/2 fl oz) water on the bottom of the oven to get a fine, crackled crust. Lower the heat to 200°C (400°F/gas 6) and bake for about 40 minutes.

potato bread

This is a moist and tasty loaf made with treacle and potatoes. It is great as a break-fast bread with butter and cheese. The dough is rather loose so it's best to let it rise in a bread basket. Don't forget to flour the basket well so the dough doesn't stick.

MAKES 2 LOAVES

800 g (1 lb 12 oz) floury potatoes

50 g (2 oz) butter

500 ml (18 fl oz) soured milk

2 tbsp bread spices (equal mix of fennel, caraway and coriander seeds crushed)

30 g (1¼ oz) fresh yeast

100 ml (3½ fl oz) treacle

1½ tbsp salt

100 ml (3½ fl oz) wheat sourdough starter

500 g (18 oz) rye flour

350-470 g (12 oz–1 lb 1 oz) strong bread flour

1. Peel the potatoes and boil until soft in lightly salted water and then let them cool. Mash with a potato masher or fork.

2. Melt the butter and mix it with the milk and spices. Warm it until the liquid is lukewarm.

3. Crumble the yeast in a mixing bowl and dissolve it in the milk. Add treacle, salt, sourdough starter and the mashed potatoes.

4. Add the flours a little at a time, and knead the dough at medium speed in a mixer for about 15 minutes, until it is soft and elastic.

5. Sprinkle with a little rye flour and let it rise in the mixing bowl under a cloth until it doubles in size, about 2 hours.

6. Preheat the oven to 250°C (500°F/gas 10).

7. Shape the dough into two round loaves and place in floured bread baskets with the smooth side down. Let rise under a cloth until they double in size, about 1½ hours.

8. Place the loaves on a tray lined with baking parchment and put them in the middle of the oven. Lower the temperature to 220°C (425°F/gas 7) and bake for about 55 minutes.

vegetable bread

This moist, spicy and filling bread is unbelievably good with a little cream cheese or spreadable goats' cheese. It's perfect as a picnic bread, with soup or with food.

MAKES 8 ROLLS

1 courgette, sliced

2 red peppers, sliced

1 red onion, sliced

3 tbsp olive oil

2 tsp curry powder

sea salt

100 g (4 oz) black olives, stoned and coarsely chopped

10 g (¼ oz) fresh yeast

350 ml (12 fl oz) lukewarm water

1 tbsp salt

4 tbsp olive oil

1 tsp golden syrup

150 ml (5 fl oz) wheat sourdough starter

100 g (4 oz) durum wheat flour

400 g (14 oz) strong bread flour

1. Preheat the oven to 250°C (500°F/gas 10).
2. Place the sliced courgettes, peppers and red onion on a tray, mix them with olive oil, curry powder and season with sea salt.
3. Roast the vegetables in the oven for about 25 minutes, until they are soft and have coloured a bit. Cool.
4. Coarsely chop the olives.
5. Crumble the yeast in a mixing bowl and dissolve it in water. Add salt, olive oil, syrup and sourdough starter.
6. Add durum flour and strong flour a little at a time and knead the dough at medium speed in a mixer for about 10 minutes, until it is soft and elastic.
7. Sprinkle with a little flour and let it rise in the mixing bowl under a cloth until it doubles in size, about 2 hours.
8. Once again preheat the oven to 250°C (500°F/gas 10).
9. Carefully fold the vegetables and olives into the dough by hand. They can stick out of the surface of the dough.
10. Divide the dough into 8 pieces and place on a tray lined with baking parchment. Let them rise under a cloth until double in size, about 1 hour.
11. Place the tray in the middle of the oven and throw 100 ml (3½ fl oz) water on the bottom of the oven to get a fine, crackled crust. Lower the heat to 200°C (400°F/gas 6) and bake for about 25–30 minutes, until they turn golden.

A typical mistake people make when baking sourdough bread is that they use too much flour in the dough. Bakers nearly always bake with a rather loose dough. The less flour there is, the lighter and airier the bread turns out, with more holes. A loose dough settles a bit while rising and of course it is a little harder to handle – it is easiest to do it on a well-floured table where you can 'shove' the bread together with a spatula. But this vegetable bread shouldn't be made with dough that is too loose since the vegetables give off quite a lot of moisture.

almond bread with dried fruit

This wonderful sourdough bread with almonds and dried fruit is a really good, luxurious breakfast bread and is also perfect with a cheese board. It is a compact bread and ought to be sliced really thin. It is also really good toasted. The loaf also lasts a long time thanks to all the fruit and almonds.

MAKES 1 LOAF

400 g dried fruit (raisins, cranberries and apricots)

25 g (1 oz) fresh yeast

300 ml (10 fl oz) lukewarm water

50 ml (2 fl oz) treacle

1¼ tbsp salt

50 ml (2 fl oz) rye sourdough starter

50 ml (2 fl oz) wheat sourdough starter

200 g (7 oz) coarse rye flour

275–325 g (9½–11 oz) strong bread flour

150 g (5 oz) flaked almonds

1. Soak the raisins and cranberries in water for 30 minutes. Drain well. Chop the apricots into small pieces.
2. Crumble the yeast in a mixing bowl and dissolve it in water. Add salt, olive oil, syrup and sourdough.
3. Add the rye flour and strong flour a little at a time. Knead the dough at medium speed in a mixer for about 12 minutes.
4. Add the fruit and almonds to the dough by hand.
5. Sprinkle with a little flour and let the dough rise in a mixing bowl under a cloth for 2–3 hours (because the dough is heavy and compact, it takes a little longer to rise).
6. Preheat the oven to 250°C (500°F/gas 10).
7. Shape the dough into a round loaf and place it on a tray lined with baking parchment. Sprinkle with flour.
8. Let rise under a cloth for about 1½ hours.
9. Place the tray in the middle of the oven and throw 100 ml (3½ fl oz) water on the bottom of the oven to get a fine, crackled crust. Lower the heat to 200°C (400°F/gas 6) and bake for about 450 minutes.

seven kinds of bagels

Bagels are a round Jewish bread (shaped like a doughnut with a hole) with roots back in the 17th century. In New York, a bagel is a typical breakfast sandwich and the myth is that it is especially good there thanks to the water, but I think it has more to do with the baker. What's special about bagels is that they are boiled before baking, which results in a chewy, compact structure. I like to serve bagels with cream cheese, thinly sliced tomato and red onion.

BASIC RECIPE

MAKES 12 BAGELS

25 g (1 oz) fresh yeast
500 ml (18 fl oz) lukewarm water
1 tbsp salt
2 tbsp honey, clear
750–850 g (1 lb 10 oz–1 lb 14 oz) strong
    bread flour
egg white for brushing

1. Dissolve the yeast in the water and add salt and honey.
2. Add flour a little at a time and mix the dough in a mixer for about 5 minutes. The dough should be firm.
3. Let the dough rise in a mixing bowl under a cloth until it doubles in size, about 50 minutes.
4. Put the dough on a floured surface and knead it lightly. Divide it into 12 pieces.
5. Shape every piece into a round shape and press out a rather large hole in the middle with your fingers. Spin the ring around your finger (like a hula hoop) to make it even.
6. Let the rings rise under a cloth on a tray lined with baking parchment for about 45 minutes.
7. Preheat the oven to 180°C (350°F/gas 4). In the meantime boil water in a large pan.
8. Boil a couple of rings at a time, 1-2 minutes on each side.
9. Dry the rings on kitchen towels and place them on a tray lined with baking parchment.
10. Brush with beaten egg white.
11. Bake in the middle of the oven for about 25 minutes.

rosemary bagels

MAKES 12 BAGELS

1 portion dough for bagels (see basic
    recipe above)
½ bunch fresh rosemary, leaved
    stripped and finely chopped
egg white for brushing
fresh rosemary and sea salt

1. Make the dough according to the basic recipe and add half of the finely chopped rosemary.
2. Preheat the oven to 180°C (350°F/gas 4).
3. Let rise, shape and boil according to the basic recipe.
4. Brush the boiled bagels with beaten egg white and sprinkle with the rest of the rosemary and a little sea salt.
5. Bake them until golden in the middle of the oven for about 25 minutes.

sesame bagels

MAKES 12 BAGELS

1 portion dough for bagels (see basic
   recipe page 170)
egg white for brushing
125 g (4 ³/₂ oz) sesame seeds

1. Make the dough according to the basic recipe.
2. Preheat the oven to 180°C (350°F/gas 4).
3. Let rise, shape and boil according to the basic recipe.
4. Brush the boiled bagels with beaten egg white and sprinkle
   with sesame seeds.
5. Bake in the middle of the oven for about 25 minutes.

blueberry bagels

MAKES 12 BAGELS

1 portion dough for bagels (see basic
   recipe page 170)
100 g (4 oz) fresh blueberries
egg white for brushing

1. Make the dough according to the basic recipe and carefully
   add the blueberries in by hand.
2. Preheat the oven to 180°C (350°F/gas 4).
3. Let rise, shape and boil according to the basic recipe.
4. Brush the boiled bagels with beaten egg white.
5. Bake in the middle of the oven for about 25 minutes.

cheese bagels

Bagels with cheese are just wonderful! It is important to choose a strong, mature and flavourful cheese such as Cheddar for the best results.

MAKES 12 BAGELS

1 portion dough for bagels (see basic recipe page 170)

250 g (9 oz) mature hard cheese (Cheddar type), coasely grated

egg white for brushing

1. Make the dough according to the basic recipe. Add two-thirds of the grated cheese to the dough and save the rest.
2. Preheat the oven to 180°C (350°F/gas 4)
3. Let rise, shape and boil according to the basic recipe.
4. Brush the boiled bagels with beaten egg white and the rest of the cheese.
5. Bake them until golden in the middle of the oven for about 25 minutes.

poppy seed bagels

There are both white and blue poppy seeds. I like to use poppy seeds in both sweet and savoury breads and they are also delicious in crumbles. You should never be stingy when using seeds because they offer such a fantastically tasty, nutty flavour.

MAKES 12 BAGELS

1 portion dough for bagels (see basic recipe page 170)

egg white for brushing

125 g (4 oz) poppy seeds

1. Make the dough according to the basic recipe.
2. Preheat the oven to 180°C (350°F/gas 4).
3. Let rise, shape and boil according to the basic recipe.
4. Brush the boiled bagels with beaten egg white and sprinkle with poppy seeds.
5. Bake in the middle of the oven for about 25 minutes.

onion bagels

Onion bagels taste mildly of onion and are beautifully decorated with red onion rings. These are perfect for the onion-lover and are great to toast.

MAKES 12 BAGELS

1 portion dough for bagels (see basic recipe page 170)

125 g (4 oz) roasted onion

egg white for brushing

2 red onions, thinly sliced

1. Make the dough according to the basic recipe and add the roasted onion to the dough.
2. Preheat the oven to 180°C (350°F/gas 4)°C.
3. Let rise, shape and boil according to the basic recipe.
4. Peel the red onions and slice thinly.
5. Brush the boiled bagels with beaten egg white and sprinkle the red onion rings over them.
6. Bake until golden in the middle of the oven for about 25 minutes.

american pie

I'm totally in love with pies. Perhaps it is because when I was little, I always sat and longed for 'Grandma Duck's pies', which I saw in comic books and in films – those pies that sat cooling in the window and that some bear always came and stole. I've dedicated this chapter to American pies, which I can't do without. Of course all are really yummy and perfect for any occasion.

shortcrust pastry

When you make a shortcrust pastry, make sure that you do not overhandle or knead the dough, otherwise you will toughen the pastry. Roll it out while it is still cold and then it'll stick together.

BASIC RECIPE
MAKES PASTRY FOR 1 PIE
150 g (5 oz) cold butter, cut into cubes
275 g (9½ oz) plain flour
30 g (oz) icing sugar
1 free-range egg, slightly beaten
½ tbsp water

1. Rub the cubed butter into the flour and icing sugar.
2. Add the egg and water and work them together just until the dough begins to stick together. Do not knead.
3. Cover the dough with clingfilm and let it rest in the refrigerator for at least 30 minutes.

aunt sally's pie

I usually make this pie in mini tins but of course you can do it as a big pie as well, in which case it will need longer in the oven. If you use frozen berries, increase the amount of corn flour you use, since the berries will release more juice as they thaw.

MAKES 6 SMALL PIES
1 portion shortcrust pastry (see basic recipe above)

FILLING
500 g (18 oz) fresh blackberries
500 g (18 oz) fresh blueberries
finely grated zest of 4 lemons
2 tbsp balsamic vinegar
250 g (9 oz) sugar
100 g (4 oz) corn flour

GLAZE
1 free-range egg, lightly beaten
1 tbsp milk
1 tbsp demerara sugar

1. Preheat the oven to 180°C (350°F/gas 4).
2. Make the shortcrust pastry according to the basic recipe.
3. Mix the blackberries and blueberries. Add grated lemon zest, balsamic vinegar, sugar and corn flour.
4. Roll out half the dough on a floured surface.
5. Cut out rounds of dough (using a small plate as a template) and press them into the pie tins, letting a little of the dough hang over the edges.
6. Add the berry filling to the pie shells.
7. Roll out the rest of the dough and make round lids for the pies. Place these over the filling and press the edges with a fork. Cut away any excess dough.
8. Brush the crust with egg whisked with milk. Sprinkle with demerara sugar and make a few incisions in each pie.
9. Bake the pies in the lower part of the oven for about 30 minutes, until they are golden. If you make just one large pie, increase the baking time somewhat.

boston apple pecan pie

I usually make this classic in the autumn, when the garden is full of tasty apples. It's simple, fast and delicious. If you don't like raisins, just leave them out.

MAKES 1 LARGE PIE OR 8 SMALL PIES

1 portion shortcrust pastry (see basic recipe page 177)

FILLING

12 large apples, peeled, cored and sliced

50 g (2 oz) butter

150 g (5 oz) brown sugar

2 tsp ground cinnamon

200 g (7 oz) almond paste, grated

juice of 1 lemon

100 g (4 oz) pecan nuts

75 g (3 oz) raisins

GLAZE

1 free-range egg, slightly beaten

1 tbsp milk

1 tbsp demerara sugar

1. Preheat the oven to 180°C (350°F/gas 4).
2. Make the shortcrust pastry according to the basic recipe.
3. Peel the apples and cut each one into thick wedges.
4. Fry the apples until soft in butter, brown sugar and cinnamon, in two batches.
5. Put the apples on a tray and let them cool.
6. Sprinkle the grate almond paste over the apples, add lemon juice, pecans and raisins, and mix.
7. Divide the pastry into two balls, one of which should be a bit bigger than the other.
8. Put the large ball on a floured surface and roll out into a circle, about 30 cm (12 inches) in diameter.
9. Roll the dough onto the rolling pin and drape over a loose-bottomed pie tin, about 24 cm (10 inches) in diameter. Carefully press the dough against the edges and let some dough hang over the edge.
10. Whisk the egg and milk and brush the edges of the dough.
11. Fill the pie shell with the apple filling and roll out the smaller piece of pastry. Slice it into strips 1½ cm (1 inch) thick and make a lattice pattern over the pie.
12. Press the strips onto the edges of the base crust and cut away any excess dough.
13. Put the pie on a tray, brush the strips with the glaze and sprinkle with demerara sugar.
14. Bake the pie in the lower part of the oven for about 35 minutes, until it is golden.

stars and stripes

I always use fresh berries in this lovely pie, otherwise the berries will release juice and the icing sugar on the raspberries will melt. If the berries are dry, the sugar will stay in place.

MAKES 1 LARGE PIE/8 SMALL PIES
1 portion shortcrust pastry (see basic recipe page 177)
100 g (4 oz) good quality white chocolate

VANILLA CREAM
500 ml (18 fl oz) milk
1 vanilla pod, seeds scraped out
150 g (5 oz) sugar
7 free-range egg yolks
75 g (3 oz) corn flour
50 g (2 oz) softened butter

125 g (4½ oz) fresh blueberries
400 g (14 oz) fresh raspberries
icing sugar to sprinkle on the pie

1. Make the shortcrust pastry according to the basic recipe (if there is leftover dough, it can be kept in the freezer).
2. Preheat the oven to 180°C (350°F/gas 4).
3. Roll out the dough and put it in a rectangular pie tin. Prick the bottom with a fork. Press a strip of aluminium foil on and over the edge of the dough so it doesn't sink down while prebaking (baking blind).
4. Prebake the pie shell in the middle of the oven for about 5 minutes, then remove the foil and bake for another 5 minutes, until it is golden.
5. Melt the white chocolate in a bowl over but not touching a pan of boiling water, then brush the chocolate over the bottom and edges of the pie shell. Let the chocolate harden.
6. Boil the milk with the vanilla seeds and the pod.
7. Whisk the sugar, yolks and corn flour until white and fluffy.
8. While whisking by hand, add the milk.
9. Pour the mixture back into the pot and warm it while whisking it vigorously. Pour it into a bowl when the mixture has really thickened. Remove the vanilla pod.
10. Melt the butter in the warm cream while whisking; continue to whisk until the cream is smooth.
11. Chill the cream in an ice bath (in a bowl placed in ice water) or in the refrigerator.
12. Powder the edges of the pie with lots of icing sugar. Spread the vanilla cream over the pie shell.
13. Place the blueberries in a square in one corner of the pie.
14. Place horizontal rows of raspberries, but leave every other row empty. Powder the raspberries until they are completely white.
15. Fill in the empty rows with the rest of the raspberries.

key lime pie

Key lime pie comes from Key West, which is a peninsula outside Miami in the US. The pie takes its name from the small, sweet limes that grow there. But you can also make this pie with regular limes. The pie is almost legendary and there are many firm opinions about how it should be made. I think it's best when it's made with condensed milk. You can bake it in one large pie tin instead of 4 small ones. A pie tin with low walls, about 22 cm (9 inches) in diameter, is just right.

MAKES 1 LARGE/4 SMALL PIES

BISCUIT BASE
200 g (7 oz) digestive biscuits, crushed
100 g (4 oz) butter, melted

FILLING
210 ml (7½ fl oz) condensed milk
4 free-range egg yolks
finely grated zest and juice of 5 limes
whipped cream and limes to serve

1. Preheat the oven to 180°C (350°F/gas 4).
2. Mix the crushed crumbs with the melted butter.
3. Press the mixture into the base and up the sides of 4 small pie tins.
4. Prebake the pie shells in the middle of the oven for about 10 minutes. Let cool.
5. Mix the condensed milk with the yolks, grated lime zest and juice. Leave the mixture to infuse and absorb the lime flavour for at least 30–60 minutes. Then strain the mixture in a fine sieve and discard the zest.
6. Fill the pie shells and bake in the middle of the oven for about 15 minutes (a little longer if making one big pie). Let cool and serve the pies with whipped cream and slices of fresh lime.

twin peaks cherry pie

When I was a teenager, I didn't miss an episode of the cult series *Twin Peaks*. Agent Cooper always had coffee and a piece of pie at the local diner. I always longed for the cherry pie. So I've come up with my own version. It's really, really good and tastes great with softened vanilla ice cream or lightly whipped cream.

1 LARGE PIE/12 SMALL PIES
1 portion shortcrust pastry (see basic recipe page 177)

FILLING
750 g (1 lb 10 oz) fresh sweet cherries, stoned
100 g (4 oz) sugar
1 vanilla pod, seeds scraped out
finely grated zest and juice of 1 lemon
2 tbsp corn flour

GLAZE
1 free-range egg, slightly beaten
1 tbsp milk
1 tbsp demerara sugar

1. Make the shortcrust pastry according to the basic recipe.
2. Preheat the oven to 180°C (350°F/gas 4).
3. Place the stoned cherries in a heavy-bottomed pot with the sugar, vanilla seeds and pod and grated lemon zest. Bring to the boil and then simmer gently.
4. Mix the lemon juice and corn flour and add it to the cherries. Whisk until the mixture has thickened. Let cool and remove the vanilla pod.
5. Divide the pastry into two portions, one of which should be a bit larger than the other.
6. Place the larger piece on a floured surface and roll it out into a round that is about 30 cm (12 inches) in diameter.
7. Roll the dough onto the rolling pin and drape it over a loose-based pie tin, about 24 cm (10 inches) in diameter. Carefully press the dough against the edges and let some dough hang over the edge.
8. Fill the pie shell with the cherry filling.
9. Roll out the smaller piece of dough into a round slightly larger than the pie tin.
10. Whisk the egg and milk and brush the edges of the dough in the pie tin. Top with the rolled-out round of pastry.
11. Pinch the edges together with your fingers and then remove any excess dough. Cut out some leaves from the extra dough and decorate the pie.
12. Place the pie on a tray, brush the whole lid with the egg mixture and attach the leaves to the middle of the top. Sprinkle with demerara sugar. Make small incisions (like sunbeams) in the top and bake the pie in the lower part of the oven for about 35 minutes, until it is golden.

mixed fruit cobbler

A cobbler is an American fruit pie that's usually made with fresh fruit or berries such as apples, peaches, blueberries or cherries. The fruit or berries are covered with a thick, undulating layer of dough that gets a lovely crust when baked. The cobbler is soft and juicy but crunchy on top. The dough is a mixture of crumble and sponge cake.

SERVES 6

COBBLER DOUGH
100 g (4 oz) butter
150 g plain flour
1 tsp vanilla sugar
1 tsp baking powder
finely grated zest of 1 lemon
1 pinch salt
50 g (2 oz) sugar
75 ml (3 fl oz) cream
50 g (2 oz) coconut flakes

FILLING
500 g (18 oz) mixed berries (currants, blueberries, raspberries)
100 g (4 oz) demerara sugar
3 peaches, thinly sliced
50 g (2 oz) flaked almonds

1. Preheat the oven to 180°C (350°F/gas 4).
2. Cube the butter into small pieces and rub it into the flour, vanilla sugar, baking powder, grated lemon zest, salt and sugar.
3. Add a little cream at a time and mix in the coconut flakes.
4. Mix the berries with the demerara sugar. Cut the peaches into segments.
5. Layer the berries, fruit and cobbler mixture in a small oven-safe dish (about 20 x 15 cm/8 x 6 inches). Sprinkle with the flaked almonds.
6. Bake in the middle of the oven for about 25 minutes until the top is golden.

american caramel pie

I serve this chewy and wonderfully caramel pie in small slices because it is so rich. Liquid glucose is a liquid sugar that you can buy in well-stocked grocery stores. You use it so the caramel doesn't crystallize and to achieve the chewy texture.

MAKES 1 LARGE PIE/12 SMALL PIES
1 portion shortcrust pastry (see basic
   recipe page 177)

FILLING
450 g (1 lb) good quality dark
   chocolate, 70% cocoa solids
200 ml (7 fl oz) double cream
200 g (7 oz) sugar
100 ml (3 ½ fl oz) water
100 ml (3 ½ fl oz) liquid glucose
1 vanilla pod, seeds scraped out
150 g (5 oz) mixed nuts (almonds,
   pecans, pistachios, and walnuts)
lightly whipped cream to serve

1. Make the pastry according to the basic recipe. If there is dough left over, it can be kept in the freezer.
2. Preheat the oven to 180°C (350°F/gas 4).
3. Roll out the dough and put it in a pie tin, about 24 cm (10 inches) in diameter. Prick the bottom with a fork.
4. Press aluminium foil around the edges of the pie shell.
5. Bake the pie shell in the middle of the oven for about 5 minutes. Remove the foil and bake for another 5 minutes until the bottom is golden. Let cool.
6. Finely chop the chocolate.
7. Melt the chocolate with the cream in a bowl over but not touching a pan of boiling water.
8. Boil the sugar, water and glucose for about 6 minutes in a large pan.
9. Add the chocolate cream and the vanilla pod and seeds to the sugar syrup and continue to boil while whisking for 10–13 minutes, until the mixture thickens and feels stiff.
10. Remove the vanilla pod and fill the pie shell with the caramel. Sprinkle with the nuts and let harden.
11. Serve the pie at room temperature with lightly whipped cream.

banana cream pie

The filling in this pie is a mixture of cream, banana and caramel sauce, which is really good. Put the pie together right before serving it, otherwise the filling makes the base damp and the bananas turn a darker colour.

MAKES 1 LARGE PIE/8 SMALL PIES
1 portion shortcrust pastry (see basic recipe page 177)

FILLING
1 tin (400 g/14 oz) condensed milk
1 vanilla pod, seeds scraped out
400 ml (14 fl oz) double cream
200 ml (7 fl oz) thick Greek yogurt
4 bananas, sliced lengthwise

CANDIED NUTS
50 g (2 oz) almonds
50 g (2 oz) walnuts
1 free-range egg white, slightly beaten
50 g (2 oz) sugar
1 tsp ground cinnamon

1. Make the pastry according to the basic recipe.
2. Make a caramel sauce with the condensed milk: place the contents in a pan and boil until a caramel consistency is reached. Let cool.
3. Preheat the oven to 180°C (350°F/gas 4).
4. Roll out the pastry and put it in a pie tin.
5. Prick the bottom with a fork. Press a strip of aluminium foil on and over the edge of the dough so it doesn't sink down while being baked.
6. Prebake the pie shell in the middle of the oven for about 5 minutes, then remove the foil and bake for another 5 minutes, until it is golden. Let the pie shell cool.
7. Split the vanilla pod and scrape out the seeds. Whisk the seeds with the cream and fold it into the yogurt.
8. Increase the oven temperature to 200°C (400°F/gas 6).
9. Mix the nuts with lightly beaten egg white.
10. Shake the nuts with sugar and cinnamon.
11. Roast them on a tray lined with baking parchment in the oven for about 10 minutes, then let cool completely.
12. Mix the cream and yogurt mixture with 2/3 of the caramel and spoon it over the pie bottom. Drizzle with the rest of the caramel.
13. Slice the bananas lengthwise and place them over the filling. Sprinkle with coarsely chopped candied nuts.

blueberry crumble with poppy seeds

I love crumble, because it is probably the world's easiest dessert. It is a really smart pie, as it is so simple to vary and flavour in different ways. I vary it with different spices, nuts, coconut flakes, seeds and of course berries. This juicy blueberry crumble has blue poppy seeds in it, and it's a great combination.

MAKES 1 PIE/6 SERVINGS

CRUMBLE DOUGH
250 g (9 oz) cold butter
150 g (5 oz) demerara sugar
175 g (6 oz) flour
25 g (1 oz) blue poppy seeds
150 g (5 oz) oatmeal

FILLING
750 g (1 lb 10 oz) frozen blueberries
100 g (4 oz) sugar
25 g (1 oz) corn flour
vanilla ice cream to serve

1. Preheat the oven to 180°C (350°F/gas 4).
2. Cube the butter into small pieces and rub together with the demerara sugar and flour until it is a crumbly dough.
3. Carefully mix in the poppy seeds and oatmeal without breaking the oatmeal too much.
4. Mix the blueberries with the sugar and corn flour and pour the filling into the bottom of an oven-safe dish.
5. Sprinkle the crumble dough over the filling and bake the pie until golden in the middle of the oven for about 25 minutes.
6. Serve warm with softened vanilla ice cream.

conversion table

Fluid Ounces	U.S. Cups	Millilitres
	1 teaspoon	5 ml
¼ ounce	2 teaspoons	7 ml
½ ounce	1 tablespoon	15 ml
1 ounce	2 tablespoons	25 ml
2 ounces	¼ cup	50 ml
4 ounces	½ cup	100 ml
5 ounces		150 ml
6 ounces	¾ cup	170 ml
8 ounces	1 cup	225 ml
9 ounces		250 ml
10 ounces	1¼ cups	300 ml
12 ounces	1½ cups	340 ml
14 ounces		400 ml
16 ounces	2 cups	450 ml
18 ounces	2¼ cups	500 ml
20 ounces	2½ cups	560 ml
24 ounces	3 cups	675 ml
25 ounces		700 ml
27 ounces	3½ cups	750 ml
30 ounces	3¾ cups	840 ml
32 ounces	4 cups	900 ml

sweet potato pie

In the US, pumpkin pie is a very common dessert for Halloween and Thanksgiving celebrations. Similar to pumpkin pie in taste and appearance, this pie is made from sweet potatoes and has a wonderful sweet, spicy but mild flavour. Of course you can also make it with pumpkin purée if you want, but make sure the purée isn't too loose and watery. It's a good idea to let some of the liquid strain away in a coffee filter.

MAKES 1 LARGE PIE/8 SMALL PIES
1 portion shortcrust pastry (see basic
   recipe page 177)

FILLING
1 large (500 g/18 oz) sweet potato
100 g (4 oz) cream cheese
50 g (2 oz) light muscovado sugar
100 g (4 oz) sugar
1 tsp vanilla sugar
1 tsp ground ginger
1 pinch ground nutmeg
½ tsp salt
2 tbsp corn flour
3 free-range eggs
2 tbsp double cream

1. Make the shortcrust pastry according to the basic recipe.
2. Preheat the oven to 180°C (350°F/gas 4).
3. Roll out the dough and put it in a fluted pie dish.
4. Peel and cube the sweet potato. Boil it until soft in lightly salted water. Drain and mix it into a smooth purée (you need about 300 ml (10 fl oz) sweet potato purée). Let it cool.
5. Whip the cream cheese, muscovado and sugar until creamy.
6. Add the sweet potato purée, vanilla sugar, ginger, nutmeg, salt and corn flour. Whip until it is completely smooth.
7. Carefully add one egg at a time, then add the cream.
8. Pour the mixture over the pie dough and bake it in the lower part of the oven until it is golden, about 30 minutes.

pasta pronto

Making your own pasta is much easier than most people believe. All you need is flour, eggs and a pasta machine. Fresh pasta can be filled with fantastic fillings or rolled out into spaghetti, linguine or shaped in other ways. Impress your guests by making your own ravioli. It's a perfect appetizer and main course served as it is with a little browned butter, black pepper and Parmesan cheese. If you want a tasty sauce, look at some of my quick and delicous pasta sauce recipes.

fresh pasta

This simple pasta dough is easy to work with in a pasta machine. The recipe makes enough pasta for 4 people and if you are making ravioli, it's enough for about 25-30 pieces, which should serve 4 to 6 depending on appetites!

BASIC RECIPE
MAKES 4 SERVINGS
325 g (11 oz) durum wheat flour
4 free-range eggs
polenta to scatter on the tray which
   holds cut pasta

1. Put the flour on a surface (see pictures on pages 202) and make a well in the middle. Break the eggs into the well and whisk into the flour with a fork a little at a time.
2. Flour your hands when the dough begins to stick and knead it until it is smooth, soft and elastic, for about 10 minutes.
3. Cover the dough with clingfilm and let it rest for at least 30 minutes in the refrigerator before rolling it out.
4. Divide the dough into 4 and roll them out one at a time. Flatten the dough with your fingers and run it through the thickest setting of the pasta machine. Continue rolling through all the settings of the machine, down to the thinnest.
5. Cut the pasta into the shape of your choice – spaghetti, tagliatelle or ravioli.
6. Boil in well-salted water until *al dente*, about 3 minutes.

saffron pasta

This tasty saffron pasta is golden yellow and beautiful with its small red saffron dots. It's fantastic in seafood dishes or with creamy sauces.

MAKES 4 SERVINGS
1 portion fresh pasta dough (see basic
   recipe above)
1 sachet (½ g) saffron threads

1. Follow the basic recipe for fresh pasta, but beat the eggs with the saffron, then let this stand a bit before you add the eggs to the flour and knead the dough together.

spinach pasta

This pasta tastes mildly of spinach and has a vibrant green colour. It's perfect for spinach ravioli if you want to go green.

MAKES 4 SERVINGS
75 g (3 oz) frozen spinach, chopped
1 portion fresh pasta dough (see basic
   recipe above)
3 free-range eggs (instead of 4)

1. Defrost the spinach and press all the liquid out by squeezing it and then pressing again through a fine sieve.
2. Follow the basic recipe for fresh pasta but use 3 eggs. Beat the eggs together with the finely chopped spinach before kneading into the dough.

six types of ravioli

It's unbelievably simple to make your own tasty ravioli, but you will need a pasta machine. Serve the ravioli with olive oil, freshly grated Parmesan cheese and black pepper. Or warm a little bit of cream seasoned with salt, pepper, lemon zest and Parmesan, and fold the pasta into it. Ravioli is also delicious if you fry the freshly boiled pillows in a little butter and serve them with a tasty pasta sauce.

BASIC METHOD
MAKES 4 SERVINGS/30 RAVIOLI
1 portion fresh pasta dough (see basic recipe page 205)
choice of filling (see variations over the following pages)
durum wheat flour to scatter on a tray

1. Make the pasta according to the basic recipe.
2. Divide the dough into 4 and roll out one at a time. Cover the other ones with clingfilm and put them in the refrigerator. Flatten the dough with your fingers and run it through the thickest setting of the pasta machine. Continue rolling through all the settings of the machine, down to the thinnest.
3. Place the whole sheet on a floured work surface.
4. Begin at one end and spoon about 1 tsp of filling on to the centre of the sheet (see photographs opposite).
5. Brush around the filling with water. Fold the sheet over the filling and carefully press all the air out. Cut out the ravioli with a pasta cutter or a sharp knife. Place them on the floured tray and immediately cover with clingfilm. Once all are cut out place the tray in the refrigerator if they are not being cooked immediately.
6. Boil the ravioli in well-salted water until *al dente*, about 3 minutes.

meat ravioli filling

FILLING FOR 30 RAVIOLI
1 bunch of parsley, finely chopped
½ garlic clove, grated
200 g (7 oz) minced beef
50 ml (2 fl oz) double cream
1 free-range egg yolk
sea salt
freshly ground black pepper

1. Mix the chopped parsley and grated garlic with the beef, cream and egg yolk and season well with salt and pepper.
2. Roll out the pasta and fill the ravioli according to the basic method above.

Filled pasta can be shaped in various ways, included these playful sweet-shaped parels. You can also make round or square pillows, crescents or shell shapes such as tortellini. You can also use a ravioli mould if you want.

sweet-shaped ravioli with butternut squash

MAKES 30 RAVIOLI

1 portion fresh pasta dough (see basic
    recipe page 205) ·
1/2 butternut squash
olive oil
sea salt
250 g (9 oz) ricotta cheese
freshly ground black pepper
a few drops truffle oil

1. Preheat the oven to 200°C (400°F/gas 6).
2. Slice the squash into segments (with the skin), drizzle with
    olive oil and season with sea salt.
3. Roast it in the oven until it is completely soft, for about
    45 minutes.
4. Let the squash cool. Remove the skin and mash with a fork.
    Add the ricotta and season with salt, pepper and truffle oil.
5. Roll out the pasta and cut rectangles, about 10 x 5 cm
    (4 x 2 in). Place a spoonful of filling in the middle of each
    rectangle and brush around the filling with water.
6. Roll it up, starting at the long side. Twist the ends so the roll
    is shaped into a sweet (see photograph opposite).

three-cheese ravioli filling

MAKES FILLING FOR 30 RAVIOLI

50 g (2 oz) Parmesan cheese, grated
50 g (2 oz) Gorgonzola cheese
250 g (9 oz) ricotta cheese
freshly ground black pepper

1. Grate the Parmesan and crumble or mash the Gorgonzola.
2. Mix the two cheeses with the ricotta and season well with
    freshly ground black pepper.
3. Roll out and fill the ravioli according to the basic method
    on page 206.

ricotta, lemon and chervil ravioli filling

MAKES FILLING FOR 30 RAVIOLI

250 g (9 oz) ricotta cheese
finely grated zest of 1 lemon
1 bunch of fresh chervil, fine chopped
sea salt
freshly ground black pepper
1 tbsp olive oil

1. Mix the ricotta cheese with the lemon zest and the finely
    chopped chervil.
2. Season with sea salt, black pepper and olive oil.
3. Roll out and fill the ravioli according to the basic method
    on page 206.

ham and basil ravioli filling

MAKES FILLING FOR 30 RAVIOLI

100 g (4 oz) smoked ham
1/2 bunch basil, finely chopped
250 g (9 oz) ricotta cheese
sea salt
freshly ground black pepper
1 tbsp olive oil

1. Finely shred the ham and add to the chopped basil. Mix with
    the ricotta and season with salt, pepper and olive oil.
2. Roll out and fill the ravioli according to the basic method
    on page 206.

ricotta and spinach ravioli filling

MAKES FILLING FOR 30 RAVIOLI
1 garlic clove, grated
75 g (3 oz) fresh baby spinach
1 tbsp butter
250 g (9 oz) ricotta cheese
sea salt
freshly ground black pepper
1 pinch nutmeg (preferably freshly
   grated)

1. Fry the spinach and grated garlic in butter very gently.
2. Squeeze the liquid out of the spinach and finely chop it.
3. Mix the spinach with the ricotta and season with salt, pepper and grated nutmeg.
4. Roll out and fill the ravioli according to the basic method on page 206.

fresh gnocchi

Gnocchi is a form of pasta made with boiled potatoes in the dough and it's simple and fast to make yourself. This pasta is at its best when fried until golden in browned butter, but first it is boiled until *al dente* like regular pasta. I like to serve it with mushrooms fried in butter.

MAKES 120 GNOCCHI/4 SERVINGS
400 g (14 oz) floury potatoes
200 g (7 oz) strong flour
1 free-range egg
1 tsp salt
butter for frying

1. Boil the potatoes in their peels in salted water until completely soft. Drain and let them cool.
2. Peel the potatoes and finely grate or press them through a potato ricer.
3. Put the flour and potato on a clean work surface and make a well in the middle. Put the egg and salt into the well.
4. Knead the flour and potato into the egg. Work the dough until smooth, about 5 minutes.
5. Boil well-salted water in a pot.
6. Divide the dough into 4, then roll each piece out on a floured surface to make a sausage shape about the thickness of a finger. Cut each sausage shape into 30 small pieces. Press every piece lightly with a fork.
7. Boil the gnocchi in salted water for a few minutes until they float up to the surface.
8. Fry the gnocchi in browned butter before serving them.

ten quick and tasty pasta sauces

vongole

This is my favourite pasta sauce – unbelievably good and simple to make with fresh vongole clams. The clams must be prepared and checked to make sure they are alive before they are boiled. Place them in very salty ice-cold water, and they will spit out any sand inside their shells. This is necessary if you don't want sand in your food. Drain the salt water and rinse the clams under cold running water. Throw out any of the clams that don't close their shells or that are open or broken.

MAKES 4 SERVINGS

1 kg (2 lb 2 oz) fresh clams
4 garlic cloves, finely chopped
1 bunch of parsley, finely chopped
½ mild red chilli, finely chopped
olive oil
3 tbsp butter
sea salt
freshly ground black pepper
50 ml (2 fl oz) white wine
finely grated zest of 1 lemon

1. Prepare the clams according to the above instructions.
2. Sweat the garlic and half of the parsley in olive oil and butter in a large pan. Add the clams without water, season with salt and pepper and stir.
3. Add the white wine, stir and cover. Steam the clams for 1 or 2 minutes, until their shells begin to open.
4. Mix in the chilli, the rest of the parsley and lemon zest.
5. Stir the sauce with freshly cooked pasta, ideally spaghetti or linguine.

Sicilian tomato sauce

MAKES 4 SERVINGS

2 tinned sardines, drained
2 garlic cloves, finely chopped
1 bunch of parsley, finely chopped
1 mild red chilli, finely chopped
olive oil
500 g (18 oz) cherry tomatoes, chopped
finely grated zest of 1 lemon
sea salt
freshly ground black pepper

1. Pour a little oil into a non-stick frying pan and fry the drained sardines and garlic slowly.
2. Add the chopped tomatoes, parsley and chilli, and stir, cooking the tomatoes until softened.
3. Add freshly cooked pasta to the pan and sprinkle the lemon zest over it. Season with salt and pepper.

saffron sauce with Spanish chorizo

I serve this really tasty bright yellow sauce at Easter, because the colour is so wonderful. The red, green and yellow in the sauce are beautiful together. Another yummy addition to this sauce is roasted red peppers – roast some little red pepper segments in the oven and serve alongside for dazzling colour.

MAKES 4 SERVINGS
200 g (7 oz) Spanish chorizo (dried)
2 garlic cloves, thinly sliced
olive oil
300 ml (10 fl oz) single cream
1 sachet (½ g) saffron
sea salt
freshly ground black pepper
200 g (7 oz) feta cheese
2 sprigs of fresh rosemary, chopped
2 handfuls of rocket, to garnish

1. Slice and fry the chorizo sausage with the thinly sliced garlic in olive oil.
2. Add the cream and saffron. Season with salt and pepper.
3. Mix the sauce with freshly cooked pasta, crumbled feta and finely chopped rosemary. Garnish each plate with a small amount of rocket.

bolognese

I serve this sauce with freshly made pasta or use it in my homemade lasagna. The chipotle, honey and vinegar add a depth of flavour that makes it extra good. I don't have much tomato in my Bolognese recipe, because I make it from a traditional recipe I was given when I lived on a vineyard in Tuscany. You never get tired of this classic.

MAKES 6-8 SERVINGS
2 onions, finely chopped
3 garlic cloves, finely chopped
½ dried chipotle (chilli), finely chopped
olive oil
1 kg (2 lb 2 oz) minced beef
sea salt
freshly ground black pepper
5 ripe tomatoes
2 tbsp butter
1 tbsp honey, clear
100 ml (3½ fl oz) water
1 chicken stock cube
1 tbsp balsamic vinegar

1. In a frying pan, soften the finely chopped onions, garlic and chipotle in the olive oil until soft and shiny. Put them into a large pan.
2. Fry the meat in two batches in olive oil and season with salt and pepper. Add this to the large pan.
3. Cube the tomatoes. Brown the butter in the frying pan, add the tomatoes and honey. Stir and let cook for 5–10 minutes. Put everything in the large pan, add water and the chicken stock cube.
4. Simmer for about 10 minutes and season with salt, pepper and vinegar.

sage sauce with vanilla

I usually serve this delicious, creamy sauce with ravioli, but it also works with grilled or poached white fish. The combination of sage and vanilla is wonderful.

MAKES 4 SERVINGS

1 vanilla pod
500 ml (18 fl oz) single cream
1 bunch of fresh sage, chopped
sea salt
freshly ground black pepper
50 g (2 oz) Parmesan cheese, grated

1. Split a vanilla pod and scrape out the seeds. Heat the pod and seeds with the cream for 3 minutes.
2. Add the chopped sage and season with sea salt and black pepper. Remove the vanilla pod.
3. Mix the sauce with freshly cooked pasta and sprinkle with grated Parmesan.

herb and dijon sauce

This is the world's fastest pasta sauce and is great with ravioli or tortellini. It's both my mother and my friends' favourite.

MAKES 4 SERVINGS

600 ml (1 pint) crème fraiche
50 g (2 oz) dijon mustard
1 bunch of tarragon, finely chopped
1 bunch of oregano, finely chopped
finely grated zest of 2 lemons
sea salt
freshly ground black pepper

1. Warm the crème fraiche and the mustard in a pan.
2. Mix in the finely chopped herbs and lemon zest. Season with salt and pepper.
3. Mix the sauce with freshly cooked pasta

cep sauce

I like to serve this fantastic sauce with pasta such as penne or rigatoni so the sauce permeates the hollows. It's a must during the mushroom season.

MAKES 4 SERVINGS

4 garlic cloves, finely sliced
400 g (14 oz) ceps, finely sliced
2 tbsp butter
sea salt
freshly ground black pepper
400 ml (14 fl oz) double cream
Parmesan cheese and rosemary to
    sprinkle over

1. Fry the cep mushrooms in butter. Add the garlic when the mushrooms have begun to get a little colour; then season with salt and pepper.
2. Pour in the cream and cook for a few minutes and then mix in to freshly cooked pasta.
3. Serve with grated Parmesan and finely chopped rosemary, sprinkled over each dish.

carbonara sauce

Pasta carbonara is a tasty, simple and fast classic. To avoid ending up with an eggy sauce, I mix it with the steaming hot, newly cooked pasta instead of warming it on the hob. In Italy, carbonara is served according to this recipe, but you can add ingredients such as green peas, haricot verts or asparagus if you want.

MAKES 4 SERVINGS
10 slices pancetta (or smoky bacon)
olive oil
3 free-range egg yolks
100 ml (3½ fl oz) double cream
200 ml (7 fl oz) milk
1 garlic clove, crushed
50 g (2 oz) Parmesan cheese, grated
sea salt
freshly ground black pepper

1. Shred the pancetta and fry it until crispy in a little olive oil, then set it aside.
2. Whisk the egg yolks, cream, milk, garlic and half of the Parmesan in a bowl. Season with salt and pepper.
3. Mix the egg mixture with hot, freshly cooked pasta and the crispy bacon.
4. Pour the pasta into a large bowl and sprinkle with the rest of the Parmesan.

Pàtes
BARONI

pomodoro sauce

I always make my tomato sauce with fresh tomatoes. The taste is so much better than if you use tinned tomatoes. This sauce is wonderful with freshly cooked spaghetti and a little buffalo mozzarella and basil. Shred the mozzarella and let it warm in the hot pasta. The sauce is also good served with grated Parmesan or Pecorino cheeses.

MAKES 4 SERVINGS
2 garlic cloves, thinly sliced
6 ripe tomatoes, diced
1 tbsp butter
1 tbsp honey, clear
1 bunch fresh oregano
1 tsp white wine vinegar
sea salt
freshly ground black pepper
buffalo mozzarella, Parmesan cheese
    and basil, to serve

1. In a pan, gently fry the sliced garlic in butter and add the honey. Stir.
2. Mix in the diced tomatoes and oregano leaves. Cook the sauce until it has a thick consistency, about 5 minutes.
3. Season with vinegar, salt and pepper.
4. Mix the sauce with freshly cooked pasta, and serve with grated Parmesan and torn shreds of buffalo mozzarella, topped with a few basil leaves.

arrabbiata sauce

Arrabbiata should be a really hot sauce made of garlic and chilli. If you can handle it, choose a strong dried chilli. Dried piri-piri gives the sauce a red-hot flavour, if that's what you want, but be careful with the amount.

MAKES 4 SERVINGS
3 garlic cloves, thinly sliced
1 mild red chilli, thinly sliced
500 g (18 oz) cherry tomatoes on
    the vine
olive oil
1 tbsp demerara sugar
sea salt
freshly ground black pepper
1 bunch of fresh parsley, finely
    chopped
finely grated zest of 1 lemon
1 tbsp white wine vinegar
Parmesan cheese, grated, to serve

1. Chop the tomatoes into quarters.
2. Warm a frying pan with olive oil and fry the garlic and chilli without letting them brown. Add the chopped tomatoes and sugar and season with salt and pepper. Stir and simmer for 2–3 minutes.
3. Add finely chopped parsley, lemon zest, vinegar and hot, freshly cooked pasta. Stir and serve with freshly grated Parmesan sprinkled over the top.

recipe index

flavour index

Love!

A big thank you to everyone who has contributed to this book.
In particular, the following fantastic people:
First and foremost I want to thank my family for everything you give me.
Thank you to Mårten, Walter, Mamma and Petronella,
who have been very engaged with this book. Johanna Karlsson,
Stephen Simmonds and Silvia Onofrio for your invaluable contributions.
Photographer Wolfgang Kleinschmidt,
graphic designer Mikael Engblom and producer Viveka Gil.
Evensen Antik, Hornsgatan 100, Garbo Interiors, Frank & Cordinata,
Gripsholm Castle and castle management,
the Royal Opera House's costume department,
Adrian Maggs and family at Villa la Casina in Tuscany.